The Scopes Trial

THE SCOPES TRIAL

A Photographic History

Introduction by Edward Caudill

Photo Captions by Edward Larson

Afterword by Jesse Fox Mayshark

THE UNIVERSITY OF TENNESSEE PRESS / KNOXVILLE

Library of Congress Cataloging-in-Publication Data

Caudill, Edward.
The Scopes trial : a photographic history / introduc-
tion by Edward Caudill; photo captions by Edward
Larson; afterword by Jesse Fox Mayshark [authors].
— 1st ed.
        p. cm.
"The photographs are from the W. C. Robinson and
Sue K. Hicks collections, Special Collections, Uni-
versity of Tennessee, Knoxville."
Includes bibliographical references.
ISBN 1-57233-080-5 (cl.: alk. paper)
ISBN 1-57233-081-3 (pbk.: alk. paper)
1. Scopes, John Thomas—Trials, litigation, etc.—
Pictorial works. 2. Evolution—Study and teaching—
Law and legislation—Tennessee—Pictorial works.
[1. Evolution—Study and teaching—Law and legis-
lation—United States—Pictorial works.] I. Larson,
Edward J. (Edward John) II. Mayshark, Jesse Fox.
III. Title.
KF224.S3 C38 1999
345.73'0288—dc21   99-050735

Contents

Acknowledgments

We are indebted to a number of people for helping us pull together the various strands of material that comprise this volume. James Lloyd, head of the University of Tennessee Special Collections, brought to our attention the availability of the photographs and agreed to help us work quickly to pull it together for publication by the seventy-fifth anniversary of the Scopes trial. Several individuals merit special thanks for their general advice and support: Richard Cornelius, curator of the Scopes Archives, Bryan College; George Webb, University of Tennessee; Ronald Numbers, University of Wisconsin–Madison; Bruce Wheeler, University of Tennessee.

EDWARD CAUDILL, University of Tennessee
EDWARD LARSON, University of Georgia

OCTOBER 1999

Introduction: The Scopes Trial

The Scopes trial, one of the greatest trials of the twentieth century, was the defining event in shaping the twentieth-century debate over science and religion.[1] In addition, it may have been the greatest calamity in Tennessee history, branding the state for generations to come as a backwater of anti-intellectualism and Bible-thumping education-haters. But "Why Dayton, of all places?" as a *St. Louis Post Dispatch* editorial asked in May 1925, perhaps a bit envious of all the attention a Tennessee town was getting. The envy from elsewhere, like the anticipated economic benefit to the local economy, was short-lived. The legacy was not.

ANTI-DARWINISM EVOLVES, AND A LAW IS CREATED

Tennessee's Butler Act was not the region's nor the state's first dalliance with anti-evolution laws. The idea was a common one in the spring of 1923, as six state legislatures considered such legislation. Only two states, Florida and Oklahoma, finally adopted anti-evolution measures. The Oklahoma legislature tagged on to its public-school textbook law a rider that declared no book should be adopted that teaches Darwinism rather than Genesis. Florida adopted a nonbinding resolution that declared it "improper and subversive" for Darwinism to be taught in public schools. William Jennings Bryan, the so-called "Great

Commoner" and leader of America's anti-Darwin crusaders, had suggested the language of the resolution, and stated that he believed no penalty should be added to the bill.[2] In 1925, the Tennessee General Assembly was less cautious in making it a crime, with a penalty, to teach evolution in public schools.

In early 1925, legislation outlawing the teaching of evolution in Tennessee public schools wound through the state legislature to little public notice, aside from a vocal minority that bothered to print pamphlets in its favor. The house passed the bill seventy-one to five on January 28. The previous year, Bryan had lectured in Nashville on "Is the Bible True?" His lecture was turned into a pamphlet and distributed to bolster the anti-evolution cause, even though it was not finding much opposition, particularly from men who would eventually face re-election in rural, conservative, religious counties.[3] For the most part, these were not professional politicians, savvy to the workings of government and policy. Legislators of the era often served for only one term, and they sought office primarily to enhance recognition in their hometowns and promote law practices or businesses.[4]

John Washington Butler, an amiable, devout farmer from rural Macon County, wrote and introduced the bill. He was a member of the Primitive Baptist Church, whose doctrinal distinction was the idea that God would not condemn a person because he or she had never heard of the gospel. A preacher sparked Butler's thinking on evolution one Sunday in 1921. During a conversation the preacher noted that a young woman from the community who had recently attended a university had returned home believing in evolution, but not in God. Butler had children, two boys and three girls, and it disturbed him that the theory of evolution was taught in Macon County schools. The next year, he ran successfully for the state legislature, taking a stand in his campaign literature against teaching evolution in public schools. As a freshman legislator, he did not introduce the legislation, but resolved to do so if re-elected in 1924.[5] Butler later said his action was based on the fairly straightforward idea that the Bible is the foundation of U.S. government and that espousing evolution means denying Christianity, thereby undermining the foundation of government.[6]

His rationale for the bill was Bryanesque:

he believed public schools should promote citizenship based upon biblical standards of morality, and evolution undermined those standards.[7] Butler's proposal differed significantly from Bryan's Florida resolution: the Florida resolution included a "balanced" approach to teaching any theory of origins; the Butler bill dealt only with evolution.

Opponents of the legislation cited freedom of expression, the scientific validity of evolution, the trial of Galileo, and the execution of Giordano Bruno. Of course, monkeys came up. One letter writer joked that the evidence for evolution was at hand—the occupants of Capitol Hill.[8] A group of thirteen Nashville ministers, mostly Methodist and Presbyterian, criticized the legislation as an assault on academic freedom and an unnecessary defense of Christianity.[9] The three main tactics for attacking the legislation had emerged: defense of individual freedom, appeal to scientific authority, and ridicule of biblical literalism. These later became the foundation for the Scopes defense.

The house acted quickly on the Butler bill: it was referred to the education committee, which on January 23 recommended its passage. Four days later, and only six days after its introduction, the full house gave final approval to the Butler bill by a vote of seventy-one to five, apparently without substantial opposition. In the senate, a parallel piece of anti-evolution legislation, introduced by Sen. John A. Shelton of Savannah, was finding a less welcome atmosphere. The senate judiciary committee on January 29 voted five to four against the bill, citing its meddling in "the question of religious belief." A few days later, on February 4, the senate judiciary committee remained consistent and defeated the house Butler bill, too. Its rejection seemed assured until senate Speaker Lew Hill of Sparta appealed for passage of the bill, pointing to petitions from teachers and women of Tennessee, and, in a bit of Bryan-esque logic, he stated that a tax-supported school should not be allowed to teach a theory that threatened a child's faith.

The senate postponed acting on the bill between February 5 and February 10, during which public attention focused on that body. The *Memphis Commercial-Appeal* lambasted the legislature for taking time to consider such bills, and the *Chattanooga Daily*

Times attacked such laws because they would weaken public confidence in the legislature and law. When the Butler bill came before the senate on February 10, the judiciary committee chairman asked that it and the Shelton measure be referred again to his committee in order to reconcile minor differences. His request was granted, and the legislature adjourned for four weeks.

The recess gave legislators the chance to gauge public opinion in their districts, and likewise gave voters a chance to pressure lawmakers. The public apparently was sufficiently informed on the anti-evolution bills, given the heavy coverage of them in newspapers across the state. The general assembly reconvened on March 9, and one day later the senate judiciary committee reversed itself, voting seven to nine to recommend senate enactment of the house-approved Butler bill. Final senate consideration of the bill started three days later. Three hours of debate included a farcical amendment to prohibit teaching that the earth is round. The Speaker ruled the amendment out of order and so directed the debate away from levity and toward a serious discussion of the proposal. The bill

finally passed on a twenty-four to six vote, and was sent to the governor for his signature.[10]

Austin Peay, the governor who signed the bill into law, was generally a progressive. He had balanced the state budget in his first term from 1922 to 1924, and in the second he spent money on schools, highways, hospitals, and prisons. He also favored extending the school year to eight months. The governor told a senator that the Butler Act was absurd and should not have been passed by the legislature. But he needed the support of rural legislators, including Butler, in order to achieve reforms. In addition, a delegation of Baptists visited him, and politics prevailed. Peay signed the act into law eight days after it passed the legislature; he seemed to both praise the bill and to be rather dismissive of it. He said he did not believe the bill would interfere with anything being taught in public schools, nor that the new law would jeopardize any teachers. He also stated that "denial of the Bible shall not be taught in our public schools."[11] As to whether it was a "serious" law or simply a symbolic action, the truth may have resided in the shadows, away from the glare of the extremes. It may have been that, as politicians, the legislators and governor were making a simple declaration to mollify some constituents, and added a one-hundred- to five-hundred-dollar fine to give the law at least the appearance of serious intent.

The Tennessee law was not enacted in a cultural vacuum, though some people, including the acerbic *Baltimore Sun* reporter H. L. Mencken, may have wanted to believe such was the case. An American Civil Liberties Union survey concerning teaching restrictions cited statutes in seven states that required daily Bible readings and forbade employment of "radical or pacifist" teachers. The survey, released in mid-1924, noted that "more restrictive laws had been enacted in the last six months than at any time in the history of the country."[12]

THE STAGE

Dayton needed an economic boost. Rhea County was chiefly agrarian, but most of the farms were small ones, with less than one hundred acres. The farms fared well enough, but businesses in Dayton were more economically depressed. A blast furnace that had em-ployed nearly a thousand men shut down in 1913, cutting the company payroll of fifty thousand dollars a month to nothing. The town withered; its population declined from about three thousand during the 1890s to fewer than eighteen hundred by July 1925.[13] In Dayton, the real issue was not evolution—it was Dayton. The trial was an unabashed ruse to promote a declining economy. "It is not a fight for evolution or against evolution, but a fight against obscurity," according to Congressman Foster V. Brown of Chattanooga.[14]

A few local citizens contrived the event in the drugstore of F. E. Robinson, also the head of the county board of education. It was there that Robinson, George W. Rappleyea, a civil engineer overseeing the local facilities for the Cumberland Coal Company, and Walter White, county superintendent of schools, were arguing on May 4, 1925, about evolution, with Rappleyea taking the pro-evolution side. When the argument resumed the next day, they asked John Scopes to come to the drug store. The twenty-four-year-old teacher had graduated from the University of Kentucky only a year earlier, and taught physics and math and coached football at Dayton. Scopes was a popular young man about town, and a good candidate for the scheme, as he was unlikely to alienate local people with radical views or activities. Although Scopes disapproved of the new anti-evolution law, he probably was not well versed in the details concerning human evolution because he did not regularly teach biology. In addition, being single meant he did not have a family that might suffer unforeseen fallout from the trial. As Scopes was drawn into the debate, he pointed out that one could not teach biology without teaching evolution. Rappleyea told Scopes that he had been breaking the law, and sprang into action. He showed Scopes a news item about the ACLU's offer to help the defense in a test case of Tennessee's new law. "That will make a big sensation," Rappleyea said. Scopes did not like the idea of being arrested, and he believed the Bible and evolution could be reconciled. But he finally relented. Rappleyea swore out a warrant against Scopes, who then was "arrested" by a local constable. Scopes then left to play tennis. He later called it a "a drugstore discussion that got past control." The lust for attention in Dayton even got to the point that some of Rappleyea's friends considered abducting him as a publicity stunt. But word got out, and the plan was abandoned when other townspeople, in a more malicious spirit, became eager to help.[15]

The ACLU agreed to help, and Scopes was charged on May 7. Dayton demonstrated numerous times its determination to nurture publicity rather than to right injustice. Daytonians protested when John Randolph Neal, chief counsel for Scopes, considered taking the trial to Chattanooga or Knoxville, either of which he felt would offer better facilities for the trial and for visitors. Townspeople even threatened to boycott Chattanooga merchants when the *Chattanooga News* attempted to stir up a new test of the law for that city. The townspeople organized a "Scopes Trial Entertainment Committee" in Dayton to arrange trial and visitor accommodations.[16] As the time for the trial neared, the town adorned shop windows with pictures of apes and monkeys, the constable's motorcycle cruised about with a "Monkeyville Police" sign, and Robinson's drugstore served "simian sodas." The "Progressive Dayton Club" approved a five-thousand-dollar fund to promote town business during the trial.[17]

THE ACTORS

Legally, the trial was inconsequential. Symbolically, it defined the science-religion debate in the twentieth century. Two strong-willed, celebrated individuals personified the extremes in the science-religion conflict—Clarence Darrow, the agnostic, and Bryan, the devout Christian. One on the political fringes with radical causes, the other a mainstream political moderate and a three-time presidential candidate.

Darrow quickly set the confrontational tone for the trial, arguing that it would be a personal challenge to Bryan and fundamentalism. One day after the ACLU accepted Darrow's offer to assist in the trial, Darrow made it clear that Bryan was on trial: "Had Mr. Bryan's ideas of what a man may do towards free thinking existed throughout history, we would still be hanging and burning witches and punishing persons who thought the earth was round."[18] Darrow saw a grand opportunity to debunk Christianity, and he later wrote that his intention was to focus the nation's attention on Bryan and fundamentalism. The ACLU was concerned that nei-

ther Scopes's civil rights nor freedom of speech greatly motivated Darrow, who saw Darwin's theory as a useful tool in his own mission against religion. Darrow's militant agnosticism concerned the ACLU's executive committee, which was not hostile to religion per se and thought Darrow could actually imperil Scope's defense. ACLU officials knew Darrow would generate bad publicity because of his agnosticism and would displease liberal, religious constituents of the organization. One ACLU attorney stated that accepting Darrow's services was a mistake because it allowed fundamentalists to portray the event as religion vs. anti-religion, which was exactly how Darrow viewed the trial. It was, for him, the pinnacle of his lifelong war on religious intolerance.[19] The accuracy of that portrayal of Darrow was best exhibited by Darrow himself when he visited Dayton a few years after the trial. Upon getting out of his car in front of the Aqua Hotel, he noticed a new church that had been completed. "I didn't do much good here after all," he was reported to have said.[20] Darrow wanted in the fight, and when he volunteered to help the defense, it was the only time in his life that he had offered legal services for free. He liked the idea of a spectacle, a street brawl between science and religion.[21] Darrow saw an opportunity to renew his attacks on the Bible and to get attention for himself. This aspect of the trial was not lost on the public and the press, which estimated that up to thirty thousand visitors would descend on Dayton for the Bryan-Darrow confrontation, though no basis was given for the figure.

During the 1920s, Darrow was one of the most famous trial lawyers in the nation. He had taken up the cause of labor in earnest during the 1890s and had gradually shifted to criminal law. His clients ranged from political radicals, including two union leaders accused in 1911 of blowing up the *Los Angeles Times* building (they eventually confessed), to wealthy murderers, with the 1924 Leopold-Loeb case being among the most spectacular in American history. Darrow saved two wealthy, intelligent Chicago teenagers from execution for the murder of a schoolmate, a crime committed apparently just to see if they could get away with it. In their defense, Darrow used arguments of psychological determinism, which reflected his repudiation of the idea of free will

and at the same time angered people who believed in individual responsibility. Such a defense reflected his personal philosophy, his agnosticism, and the delight he took in challenging traditional concepts of morality and religion. He was, as one historian put it, "the last of the 'village atheists' on a national scale."[22] Darrow spent his life ridiculing Christianity— in the courtroom, on the Chautauqua circuit, during public debates and lectures, and in books and articles for popular audiences. He believed the biblical concepts of salvation and original sin were not only dangerous, but "silly, impossible and wicked."[23] Thus, Darwin was most helpful in Darrow's crusade against divine creation and purpose in nature. When the anti-evolution crusade erupted, Darrow saw an opportunity to renew his legal attacks on the Bible.

History too often diminishes losers, as has been the case with Bryan. The popular image of him is commonly that of the vanquished fool, as portrayed in the film *Inherit the Wind,* which demonizes Bryan and lionizes Darrow. As the Democratic nominee for president three times and secretary of state under Woodrow Wilson, Bryan was a national figure. He was a decisive loser in three presidential campaigns in 1896, 1900, and 1908, claiming 45–48 percent of the popular vote. This was a part of Darrow's grudge against Bryan, whom Darrow blamed for the misfortunes of the Democratic Party, which became a minority party at the presidential level until the 1930s (excepting the election of Woodrow Wilson, which had occurred only because Theodore Roosevelt and William H. Taft split the Republican vote in 1912). In Tennessee, Bryan had fared better, winning 52–53 percent of the vote in those same elections. He had started his national political career with election to Congress in 1890. Perhaps his greatest moment came in 1896 with his "Cross of Gold" speech, delivered to the Democratic National Convention in defiance of the party's conservative leader, Grover Cleveland. In the address, he demanded an alternative silver-based currency to help debtors who were struggling under deflation caused by reliance on limited gold-backed money. He drew on religious imagery and appeal to the majority, two ideas to which he remained committed throughout his life. The speech also won the party's presidential nomination for him. He lost the election, but continued to fight, focusing his attack on imperialism and militarism in the wake of the Spanish-American War, and battling for increased regulation of corporations.

His attacks on evolution established him by spring 1921 as the national leader of anti-evolutionists. As he focused on what he deemed the speculative nature of evolution, Bryan also redefined fundamentalism as anti-evolutionism, claiming that the theory put faith in random chance rather than in God. In a letter to the *Chicago Evening Post*, Bryan detailed what he believed to be unscientific about evolution. First, he wrote, Darwin's theory was merely a hypothesis, which Bryan said was a scientific synonym for a "guess"; second, the theory lacked incontrovertible evidence; third, scientists had documented no instances of one species changing into another. It followed, he concluded, that such speculation should not be taught in public schools.[24] Bryan's attempt to challenge evolution scientifically was important because fundamentalists could not deny the significance of science. Their challenge would be more effective if it were scientific rather than theological.

In 1921, when Bryan began his crusade in earnest against Darwinism, he was on the campaign stump again. He traveled across the country, giving hundreds of speeches, including major addresses to nine different legislatures in the South and Midwest, pressing his case in dozens of popular books and articles, including articles in the *New York Times* and *Chicago Tribune*. He reached an estimated fifteen million readers with his syndicated column, "Weekly Bible Talks," as he personally lobbied politicians, school officials, and public figures. The years of campaigning made him an ideal actor in the Scopes trial in one respect: he was a celebrity and would attract attention. However, he had not been active in trial law for thirty years.

Throughout his life Bryan maintained faith in God and in the people. The apparently disparate strands of thought and action—the liberal reformer combined with the conservative fundamentalist—were not contradictory because both his anti-evolutionism and progressivism supported reform, appealed to majoritarianism, and were based on his Christian convictions. It was the social consequences of Darwin, in particular, that disturbed Bryan:

"The Darwinian theory represents man as reaching his present perfection by the operation of the law of hate—the merciless law by which the strong crowd out and kill off the weak."[25] It followed, Bryan believed, that such a social view was an obstacle to reform: if people were simply slaves to their animal natures, reform was pointless. He had seen such views used to bolster conservative politics and economics in earlier decades, and he argued that the view of humanity offered in Darwin's *Descent of Man* "would weaken the cause of democracy and strengthen class pride and power of wealth."[26] The decline of progressivism after World War I was a catalyst in Bryan's campaign against Darwinism, which he also blamed for the public's generally apathetic view of reform after the war. The political reformer and the fundamentalist preacher in Bryan both found a common enemy in evolution for eroding faith in God, which in turn discouraged altruistic efforts as people came to accept the world as it is rather than building a better one via social reform.[27] His strong opposition to teaching evolution in public schools was grounded in his populist politics. He distrusted intellectuals, which included scientists, and it was simply the right of taxpayers to decide what should be taught in their schools.[28] Walter Lippmann may have summed up Bryan's apparently paradoxical sides as a reformer and reactionary: "The spiritual doctrine that all men will stand at last equal before the throne of God meant to him that all men are equally good biologists before the ballot box of Tennessee."[29]

Bryan's opposition to evolution was limited, and that opposition began in earnest with the theory's inevitable challenge to the idea of supernatural creation of humans. In his first public address on Darwinism in 1904, Bryan stated, "I have the right to assume a Designer back of the design [in nature]—a Creator back of the creation; and no matter how long you draw out the process of creation; so long as God stands back of it you can not shake my faith in Jehovah."[30] This allowed for an "old earth" and even for limited evolution, but not for the evolution of humanity. The speech was delivered regularly in the early part of the century, but Bryan said little on the subject until the 1920s, when he blamed Darwinism for World War I and a decline in faith among educated Americans.

Even as late as 1923, Bryan was not anti-evolution. Working with the Florida legislature on a nonbinding resolution against teaching evolution, Bryan noted that the objection was not to teaching evolution as a hypothesis, but to teaching it as a proven fact,[31] and he agreed with the resolution's focus on human origins. In his "Menace of Darwinism" speech, first given in 1921, Bryan said the primary concern was "protecting man from the demoralization involved in accepting a brute ancestry." He allowed that plant and animal life, "up to the highest form of animal might, if there were proof of it, be admitted without raising a presumption that would compel us to give a brute origin to man."[32] He saw natural selection as a threat to belief in God and to social order by its justification of a simplistic social Darwinism in which society's strong eradicated the weaker members. The "Menace of Darwinism" speech evolved into a book, *In His Image*, published in 1922, in which Bryan assailed Darwinism as not only irreligious, but unscientific, "guesses strung together."[33] In Bryan's undelivered final statement on evolution—he died before he had a chance to publish it or deliver it in full—the

Commoner challenged evolution both on the basis of religion and science. It was, he said, "an insolent minority [trying] to force irreligion upon the children. . . ."[34] In particular, Bryan said, the teaching of evolution was a threat to young people: "Whatever may be said in favor of teaching evolution to adults, it surely is not proper to teach it to children who are not yet able to think. . . . And yet, the school children are asked to accept guesses and build a philosophy of life upon them. . . ."[35]

Ultimately, Bryan demanded in the statement that one accept either evolution or Christianity—but not both. This, according to Ginger, was the "great mischief" done by Bryan and the fundamentalists, forcing people into an either-or choice. Given such a choice, most people would come down on the side of God.[36] The issue was more complex than simply God or Darwin, and the either-or simplicity masked a number of problems facing Protestantism in the 1920s. According to Szasz, evolution was only one of several major issues confronting Protestants. There was growing concern among church conservatives, whose leadership became increasingly aggressive, that liberalism was growing too strong in many denominations. In addition, many Christians saw World War I and its aftermath as a failure of the hopes of Christianity.[37] Evolution eventually came to dominate all other issues that were part of the conservative revolt against liberal Christianity. Many conservatives were displeased with the elevation of evolution to such primary status, as they felt it caused the real theological issues to be lost. The editor of the *Watchman Examiner* in 1925 bemoaned the fact that the Scopes trial and evolution ever became an issue for fundamentalists. Ultimately, it did become central to fundamentalism, as evolution grew into a symbol, for many, of the nation's ills.[38]

In the battle for anti-evolution legislation, Bryan was faithful to the tenets that had guided him throughout his public life: Christian morality and majority rule. Addressing the West Virginia legislature in 1923, Bryan argued that public schools were compelled to teach what the public wanted them to teach: "The hand that writes the pay check rules the school."[39] By his own estimate, 90 percent of Americans agreed with his position on evolution, so he was simply representing the will of the people, in whom he trusted.[40]

THE ACLU

Bryan and religion drew Darrow into the trial, but religion itself was not one of the factors that brought the ACLU into the case. In fact, Quakers helped found and finance it during World War I as a means of protecting religiously motivated pacifists from compulsory military service. While Bryan was espousing the inevitable correctness of the majority's decision, the ACLU was growing more suspicious of the idea. During the First World War, the postal service banned from the mail twelve different antiwar pamphlets produced by the National Civil Liberties Bureau, predecessor of the ACLU. Darrow worked with the bureau, albeit unsuccessfully, to negotiate a settlement. The bureau later defended the radical Industrial Workers of the World, and federal agents started spying on the bureau. In addition the NCLB's leader, Roger Baldwin, soon was jailed for refusing to comply with the Selective Service Act. Such experiences changed the organization's view of and trust in majority rule.

The rise of Bolshevism and subsequent hysteria provoked rapid and harsh government reaction, which included laws against violent or unlawful activities designed to disrupt government or commerce. The political activism came at a time of labor unrest, and the two often went hand in hand. The bureau changed its name to the American Civil Liberties Union to reflect its new emphasis on violations of civil liberty, which they saw as often related to union activity. The ACLU considered public school teachers a part of the labor movement. A new sensitivity to civil rights and tyranny by the majority deeply influenced the ACLU's approach to the anti-evolution crusade.[41]

Liberal, elitist New Yorkers dominated the organization, and the anti-evolution crusade was just one of the popular movements to restrict academic freedom that the ACLU opposed. The organization fared poorly in courtroom efforts to defend labor and conscientious objectors—so poorly that it was still looking for its first court victory at the time of the Scopes trial. As a result the ACLU had resorted increasingly to action designed to influence public opinion. Generating publicity was a common tactic among early civil rights groups, which included the National

Association for the Advancement of Colored People, the Anti-Defamation League, and the American Jewish Congress. It was an approach that heavily influenced the ACLU's approach to the Tennessee case.

The ACLU first offered to defend public school teachers' free-speech rights in 1924 and in that statement added anti-evolution laws as a chief issue, along with the dismissal of teachers who expressed political views outside the classroom. The ACLU had been tracking anti-evolution laws in several states when the Tennessee legislature passed and the governor signed into the law the Butler Act. The ACLU immediately sent to Tennessee newspapers a press release, offering to defend any teachers prosecuted under the law.[42]

BRYAN ON TRIAL

The event spanned only twelve days, opening Friday, July 10, with jury selection and ending Tuesday, July 21, with Scopes's conviction. The carnival atmosphere had been building well before the actual start of the trial. When it began, the town was decorated with banners, as people packed the court-house for the spectacle, and merchants moved to make a quick profit. On that Friday, as action began in earnest to try Scopes and publicize Dayton, the courtroom filled with spectators, reporters, and lawyers. Judge John Raulston had to delay action because of doubts about the grand jury indictment, issued in May, against Scopes. The indictment had been acquired quite hastily, out of fear of being beaten to the stunt by another community. So the judge empanelled a new grand jury, which prepared to hear the case. But the witnesses against Scopes, three of his students, aged between fourteen and fifteen years old, were concerned about getting him in trouble. So they headed for the woods. Scopes found them and brought them back, and he was finally indicted before the morning ended.

It took only two and oné-half hours to select a jury of twelve men for the trial itself, and attorneys questioned only nineteen men to find those twelve. One of the nineteen admitted to being illiterate, and three others testified they read only the Bible. Judge Raulston delayed opening court on Monday so radio hook-ups could be adjusted, as he took pride in the fact that it was the first trial ever to be broadcast. Prosecutors offered their opening remarks, and Darrow castigated Bryan, "the man from Florida," for his part in the "foolish, mischievous and wicked act."[43] And so one of the themes of the trial was presented: Darrow versus Bryan. According to Ginger, the prosecution and the defense argued throughout the trial about what the Butler Act prohibited. The defense said it forbade teaching evolution and teaching that humanity evolved from lower animals; the prosecution said it only prohibited teaching evolution.[44] The defense worked to focus the issue on teaching a story of human origins that collided with the Genesis account. The prosecution maintained the issue was simply whether or not Scopes had violated the Butler Act, or, in other words, did he teach evolution?

The first witness for the state, Walter White, superintendent of Rhea County schools, testified that Scopes had said in May that he could not teach the biology text without teaching evolution. He was followed on the witness stand by a fourteen-year-old student of Scopes's, then by a seventeen-year-old student of Scopes's. From cross-examining them, Darrow confirmed the fact that Scopes had indeed taught from the offending text. The state's fourth witness was druggist F. E. Robinson, who recounted that Scopes and Rappleyea had discussed the Butler Act, that Scopes admitted to teaching evolution, and that Scopes had asserted no one could teach biology without violating the law. Darrow had fun with the witness as he pointed out that Robinson, the head of the school board, was selling the offending text in his drugstore. He jokingly advised Robinson that he was not bound to answer some of the questions because of the constitutional ban on self-incrimination.[45]

In arguing over the admissibility of expert testimony by scientists, Bryan managed to sidetrack himself onto a long assault on evolution. Though it was not Bryan at his rhetorical finest, he did hold the audience's attention. His basic legal argument was that expert testimony was irrelevant because such experts could not defeat the will of the people, which was expressed in the Butler Act. His evangelical roots reasserted themselves as he lambasted the idea of evolution: "The Christian believes man came from above, but the evolutionist believes he must have come from below!" Prosecutor Dudley Field Malone, in response, challenged anyone to claim that it was not a religious issue that was before the court. And, furthermore, he exhorted, "We feel we stand with fundamental freedom in America. . . . We ask your honor to admit the evidence as a matter of correct law, as a matter of sound procedure and as a matter of justice to the defendant." The *New York Times* called it the "greatest debate on science and religion in recent years" and reprinted the speeches by Bryan and Malone.[46] When court reconvened the next morning, a Friday, it met only long enough for Raulston to rule against the defense. Many thought the case was over, as court was recessed until Monday in order to give the defense time to prepare witness statements for the appellate review. Many journalists were leaving town that weekend as Darrow planned for Monday. If he could not call scientific experts to the stand, he was going to call an expert on the Bible—William Jennings Bryan himself.

The high point of the trial was Darrow's grilling of Bryan about his literal interpretation of the Bible. It has become the stuff of legend. Darrow was merciless in cross-examining Bryan about his reading of the Bible and about his lack of knowledge concerning science. A few excerpts from the trial transcript:

Mr. Darrow: You believe the story of the flood to be a literal interpretation? When was that flood?

Mr. Bryan: I wouldn't attempt to fix the date. The date is fixed, as suggested this morning.

Mr. Darrow: About 4004 B.C.?

Mr. Bryan: That has been the estimate. I would not say it is accurate.

Mr. Darrow: That is the estimate printed in the Bible.

Mr. Bryan: Everybody knows that—at least I think most of the people know—that was the estimate given.

Mr. Darrow: But what do you think that the Bible itself says? Don't you know how it is arrived at?

Mr. Bryan: I never made a calculation.

Mr. Darrow: A calculation from what?

Mr. Bryan: I could not say.

Mr. Darrow: From the generations of man?

Mr. Bryan: I would not want to say that.

. . . .

Mr. Darrow: . . . Do you know anything about how many people there were in Egypt 3,500 years ago, or how many people there were in China 5,000 years ago?

Mr. Bryan: No.

Mr. Darrow: Have you ever tried to find out?

Mr. Bryan: No sir; you are the first man I ever heard of who was interested in it. (laughter)

Mr. Darrow: Mr. Bryan, am I the first man you ever heard of who has been interested in the age of human societies and primitive man?

Mr. Bryan: You are the first man I ever heard speak of the number of people at these different periods.

Mr. Darrow: Where have you lived all your life?

Mr. Bryan: Not near you. (laughter and applause)

Mr. Darrow: Nor near anybody of learning?

. . . .

Mr. Darrow: Have you any idea of the length of the periods [the days in Genesis]?

Mr. Bryan: No, I don't.

Mr. Darrow: Do you think the sun was made on the fourth day?

Mr. Bryan: Yes.

Mr. Darrow: And they had evening and morning without the sun?

Mr. Bryan: I am simply saying it was a period.

Mr. Darrow: They had evening and morning for four periods without the sun, do you think?

Mr. Bryan: I believe in creation, as there told, and if I am not able to explain it, I will accept it. . . .[47]

And so it went for Bryan, who was not a biblical literalist, but was made to appear to be defending literalism during the ninety-minute exchange. He must have disappointed some of his followers with the admission that the six days of creation described in Genesis were probably not literal days, and that describing Joshua as making the sun stand still was simply using language and images that people of the time could understand. He had blundered in agreeing to be questioned, but characterized his action during the testimony as being a defense of revealed religion. Darrow's purpose, Bryan charged, was simply to "slur . . . the Bible." Darrow angrily retorted: "I am examining you on your fool ideas that no intelligent Christian on earth believes."

Despite Bryan's testimony, Scopes was convicted and fined one hundred dollars. On Sunday, July 26, five days after the conclusion of the trial, Bryan made his most significant contribution to the anti-evolution cause. He died. In the days following the trial, Bryan worked on polishing and expanding an anti-evolution speech—the "final statement" quoted earlier—which he had arranged to be published in the *Chattanooga News*. On Saturday, he delivered part of the speech to crowds in Jasper and Winchester, to an enthusiastic response each time. He returned to Dayton on Sunday, led a prayer at the Methodist Church, South, and returned to a private residence where he had stayed during the trial. After lunch, he took a nap, and died in his sleep. He became a martyr for the cause.[48] Mencken quipped, "We killed the son-of-a-bitch,"[49] but it was a botched slaying, because Bryan's death gave new life to his ideas and beliefs. Shortly after his death, efforts were underway to build a university in Dayton based on fundamentalist theology and as a memorial to Bryan. Bryan College started in 1930. In a further touch of irony, its first classes were held in the old Rhea County High School, the scene of Scopes's crime.

In a tactical error, the defense agreed to let the judge fix the penalty, but the state constitution required that the jury impose the penalty. On appeal, the Tennessee Supreme Court seized upon that technicality to reverse the judgment against Scopes. Thus, there was no case to take to the U.S. Supreme Court, as the defense had desired. In the written opinion, the chief justice stated, "We see nothing to be gained by prolonging the life of this bizarre case." He suggested that the attorney general drop the case rather than retry Scopes. The chief justice noted that dropping the case might help restore some dignity to the state.[50]

AFTER THE TRIAL

Within a few years of the trial, the anti-evolution fervor had subsided everywhere except in Arkansas, where an anti-evolution bill was passed in 1927. But it met with firm resistance from University of Arkansas students. Members of a student organization stated, "We do not want to be laughed at, as are the graduates of the University of Tennessee, and practically boycotted by the larger universities and medical schools when we seek to pursue our education further." Oklahoma had passed anti-evolution legislation in 1923, but repealed it in 1925. Similar bills were defeated in 1927 in Florida, Delaware, West Virginia, California, North Dakota, Minnesota, New Hampshire and Maine, and in 1926 in Virginia.[51] Tennessee held out.

The first attempt to repeal the Butler Act was in 1935, but by a vote of sixty-seven to twenty the state house left the law in place.

In 1952, the repeal effort failed again, in part due to the efforts of Bryan College to keep it in place.[52] In 1959 the Middle Tennessee State University chapter of the American Association of University Professors petitioned the legislature for repeal of the act. The Rutherford County Court condemned such "free-thinking" educators, and said the "God-fearing men" of the court deplored action against the anti-evolution law. Another state official argued that a biology professor who had urged repeal of the law should look for employment elsewhere if he could not abide by the laws of Tennessee.[53] The Butler Act finally was repealed in 1967. But the fight was not over. In 1974, Tennessee lawmakers required equal emphasis be given in biology texts for various theories of origins. The alternatives, in particular, meant the Genesis account. Arkansas and Louisiana enacted similar legislation in 1981.[54]

THE LEGACY

Dayton annually celebrates the trial. There is a Scopes Trial Museum in the old courthouse. In addition, fame returns periodically to the trial's site. In 1960, the city hosted the world premiere of *Inherit the Wind*; in 1972, another film, *The Darwin Adventure,* premiered in Dayton; a 1974 symposium, with professors of law, history, and biology, was held in the courtroom; and *Inherit the Wind* has been staged a number of times at the courthouse.

In the 1990s, Tennessee legislators still haggled over the issues of the Scopes trial. In early 1996, the Tennessee General Assembly attracted national and international attention— even a visit from the British Broadcasting Corporation—with debate over a bill prohibiting the teaching of evolution as a "fact," rather than as a theory.[55] The senate defeated the bill after five hours of debate. It was a religion vs. science issue, in spite of the bill's wording, which made no reference to religion. The bill stated: "No teacher or administrator in a local education agency shall teach the theory of evolution except as a scientific theory." The law under which Scopes was prosecuted made it illegal to teach humanity's descent from a "lower order of animals" or "any theory that denies the story of divine creation of man as taught in the Bible."[56] Legislation requiring the posting of the Ten

Commandments also has been debated in Nashville in recent years. Though not dealing with evolution directly, it is a member of the same species of laws that do.

Like life itself, the controversy does not simply stop, but keeps evolving. One historian summarized the consequences of the trial a few decades after it ended: "The drugstore loafers had accomplished their purpose. Dayton was on the map and Tennessee had become the laughing stock of much of the western world."[57]

A fundamentalist died in Dayton in 1925, but fundamentalism did not. Scopes lost in Dayton, but not science.

A Photographic History

Dayton, Tennessee, as seen at the time of the Scopes trial in July 1925, from Buzzard's Point or Walton Ridge. Situated in the Tennessee River valley between Chattanooga and Knoxville, Dayton grew from a village of two hundred people in 1880 to a small city of nearly three thousand by 1890 following the construction of a Southern Railway line through the valley. The railroad opened the region to national commerce, facilitating the development of agriculture and mining, with Dayton becoming the governmental and commercial center for surrounding Rhea County. The construction of a new blast furnace in Dayton for processing local iron ore spurred the town's growth. By 1925, however, the county was probably best known for its strawberries, which local farmers grew in great numbers and shipped in refrigerated railcars to northern markets in the late spring and early summer.

In this closer view from July 1925, Dayton resembled many other rural American towns of the period. The surface calm masked a faltering economy, however, especially after the blast furnace closed early in the century. The town's population had dropped to approximately eighteen hundred people. Dayton continued to serve as the trading center for a prosperous agricultural region, but local civic leaders began actively courting new industry to improve the community's economy. During the still prosperous Roaring Twenties, they dreamed and schemed of making their town more than just another farming community. To that end, they opened a new high school at a time when many Tennessee towns still only offered elementary education.

Market Street was Dayton's main commercial thoroughfare in July 1925. As shown in this photograph taken at the time, one- and two-story storefronts lined the street for several blocks downtown. Market Street stores sold all the basic necessities, including cloths and other dry goods, hardware, books, and groceries. Banks, hotels, pharmacies, and restaurants also fronted on this street. Some of the buildings were made of brick, but most of wood. Although automobiles, particularly the popular Model-T Ford, had become the most common means of transportation, horse-drawn farm wagons remained a common sight on the street. Most of Dayton's roads were unpaved, and turned into avenues of mud in heavy rainstorms. Market Street boasted wide, raised sidewalks and street-lights, but there were no stoplights in town. City officials closed a portion of Market Street to vehicle traffic during the Scopes trial, creating a pedestrian mall for street vendors, carnival games, and the crowds of persons attracted to Dayton for the court proceedings.

Dayton boasted a new high school at the time of the Scopes trial in 1925. The school, shown in this photograph, served students from throughout the county, but mostly attracted students from the town of Dayton. At the time, many rural Tennessee children obtained only an elementary-school education. John Scopes taught in this building as a new teacher— his first job after graduating from college in 1924. He came to Dayton to take the teaching job, having been born in Illinois and educated at the University of Kentucky. Scopes taught general science and mathematics, mostly to younger students. He also coached the school's football team. Although high school football did not yet dominate small-town community events in Tennessee, as it would later in the twentieth century, it was growing in popularity. As a football coach, Scopes was better known within the community than most non-native teachers at the new high school. He was generally well-liked by students, parents, and townspeople.

In 1925, Dayton's leading pharmacy was owned and operated by Fred E. Robinson on Market Street. A respected local leader, Robinson served as president of the Rhea County School Board at the time of the Scopes trial. On May 4, 1925, after reading about the ACLU's offer to defend any schoolteacher willing to challenge in court a controversial new Tennessee law against teaching evolution, Robinson and other local civic leaders decided to initiate such a lawsuit as a means of attracting attention to Dayton. They hatched their plan at the soda fountain of Robinson's downtown drugstore, shown in this 1925 photograph. The conspirators included school superintendent Walter White, city attorneys Herbert and Sue Hicks, local mine manager George Rappleyea, and others. Only after deciding to bring the lawsuit did they summon high-school science teacher John Scopes to the drugstore and ask him to serve as the defendant. Although he did not teach biology, Scopes opposed the new anti-evolution statute and agreed to participate in the test case.

The pending trial became front-page news across the United States soon after John Scopes was indicted on May 5, 1925. Out-of-town reporters and curious visitors soon descended on Dayton to write about or observe the spectacle of a teacher on trial for teaching a recognized scientific theory. Fred Robinson attempted to capitalize on the situation almost immediately by proudly advertising his drug store as the place "WHERE IT STARTED." He strung a banner with those words across Market Street, with a hand pointing to his store. No need to explain what "IT" meant—the pending trial was the principal topic of discussion in Dayton. When news photographers came to town to take pictures, the banner pointed them toward Robinson's Drug Store, where Scopes and town officials willingly posed for photos seated around the soda-fountain table "where it started."

Interest in the pending Scopes trial grew as two of America's most prominent public figures—William Jennings Bryan and Clarence Darrow—volunteered to participate in the event on opposing sides. A three-time nominee of the Democratic Party for president and former secretary of state, Bryan attracted the most attention when he offered to join the prosecution. He commanded a widespread following both for his progressive political views and conservative religious ones. Although Bryan had served as a county prosecuting attorney early in his political career, by the twenties he was best known as an orator. He delivered an average of over two hundred speeches, addresses, and lectures per year throughout his later life. Any Bryan speech caused a stir, but his appearance at Dayton to defend the right of the public to ban the teaching of evolution in tax-supported schools created a sensation. His nationwide advocacy of such restrictions had laid the foundation for enactment of Tennessee's 1925 anti-evolution statute, and now he came to defend it in court. Townspeople and visitors in Dayton anticipated his arrival on July 7, 1925, three days before the trial began. This picture shows the crowd assembling early at Dayton's railroad station, awaiting the arrival of the Royal Palm Limited carrying Bryan to Dayton from his home in Miami. The express train made a special stop to deliver Bryan; it usually passed through town without stopping.

William Jennings Bryan received a hero's welcome when he stepped off the train in Dayton for the Scopes trial. Some newspaper reporters estimated the crowd at up to one thousand persons, or over half the town's population. A band played popular patriotic and religious songs. Civic leaders were on hand to greet the man known throughout America as the "Great Commoner." Everyone wanted to shake his hand. His wife received flowers and hugs. Bryan wore a tropical pith helmet to protect his balding head from the summer sun and, some suggested at the time, to stand out in the crush of humanity. Like the seasoned politician he was, Bryan passed through town on his way from the train station to his temporary residence at the home of Dayton druggist F. R. Rogers, greeting well-wishers and talking to reporters along the route. He delivered a clear and consistent message: Belief in human evolution so greatly undermines religion and morality that the legislature should ban its teaching in public schools.

The arrival in Dayton of Clarence Darrow as Scopes's chief defense attorney was also greatly anticipated. Although he arrived in town by private automobile without advance notice on July 9, 1925, he soon took to the town streets and was immediately recognized. Darrow appears at the center of this photograph, looking toward the camera, surrounded by a crowd of townspeople and visitors. At the time, Darrow stood out as America's most famous trial attorney. He retained his office in Chicago but carried on a truly nationwide legal practice. Darrow was particularly well known for defending persons accused of notorious crimes. In these highly publicized trials, he pioneered the use of jury selection as a means to win acquittals and became famous for his eloquent closing arguments and effective cross-examination of witnesses. Darrow's courtroom oratory led to a second career as a speaker. This added to his notoriety, because he typically used his oratory to defend unpopular causes—particularly free thought against religious orthodoxy—just as he used his courtroom skills to defend notorious defendants.

Clarence Darrow recognized the need for good public relations in the Scopes trial just as much as Bryan did. Like Bryan, Darrow made a point of circulating among townspeople in Dayton and talking with the assembled reporters. He created media opportunities whenever possible. In this scene staged for news photographers, Darrow (right center, wearing hat) greets John Scopes (left center, facing Darrow) upon Darrow's arrival in Dayton for the trial. Scopes's local attorney, John R. Neal of Knoxville, a supporter of teaching evolution, leans between Scopes and Darrow. A journalist stands to Darrow's left at this railroad-station welcome of the Chicago attorney by his Dayton client. Interested spectators watch from behind. Although this meeting between Darrow and Scopes was portrayed in some press accounts as being the first between the lone Tennessee defendant and his famous legal defender, the two had actually met in both New York City and Dayton prior to the trial. Further, Scopes had been on hand when Darrow had first driven into town, several hours before this staged greeting.

George Rappleyea, pictured here during the Scopes trial, originally instigated the idea of challenging Tennessee's new anti-evolution statute by staging a criminal prosecution of a local schoolteacher. Rappleyea had recently moved to Dayton from New York to oversee the largely dormant local ironworks for their northern owners. Trained in civil engineering at Ohio Northern University, Rappleyea had drifted away from the Catholicism of his childhood and fully accepted the theory of human evolution. When the Tennessee legislature debated legislation to outlaw the teaching of human evolution, he wrote a letter to the *Chattanooga Times* ridiculing the proposal. Later, after the Butler bill passed, he hit upon the idea of testing the new law in court after learning of an offer by the New York–based American Civil Liberties Union to defend any schoolteacher willing to challenge it. Rappleyea then persuaded local civic leaders that staging the test case could help put their town on the map. Together, they asked Scopes to serve as the defendant. Throughout the trial, Rappleyea stood out as Scopes's most visible and vocal local supporter. Rappleyea also served as the local host for defense attorneys and expert witnesses. He typically sat with the defense counsel at the trial and regularly spoke to reporters.

John Scopes posed for this stylistic photograph during his trial in Dayton, Tennessee, for violating a new state law against teaching about the theory of human evolution in public school. Scopes had just completed his first year as a general science instructor in Dayton. He later confirmed the persistent rumor that he had never actually violated the law. He simply agreed to test it at the request of Dayton civic leaders, including the president of the county school board. When these leaders summoned him away from a tennis game to ask him to serve as the defendant in a judicial test of the new law, Scopes indicated that he once substituted for the regular biology teacher. The required biology textbook, which Scopes had used on this occasion, featured an evolutionary explanation of human origins. To avoid any further questions on this point, Scopes never testified at trial and the defense never raised the issue. The law itself, rather than the defendant, was really on trial. Violating it only carried a small monetary penalty anyway, which others paid on Scopes's behalf. Scopes was never jailed or threatened with jail and could have remained a teacher in Dayton after the trial, but instead accepted a scholarship to study geology at the University of Chicago. He later became a petroleum engineer and managed an oil refinery in Louisiana.

Defense counsel Clarence Darrow, age sixty-eight, sat for this photograph in the courtroom during the Scopes trial. By this point in his illustrious career, many Americans recognized Darrow's leather-like face, serious scowl, unruly hair, and piercing eyes. He continued to wear wide suspenders after they passed out of style and generally cultivated a casual, informal image that played on his roots in a small Ohio farm town during the nineteenth century. His image served him well before juries and public audiences, especially when he argued for rich defendants or unpopular causes. Darrow did both throughout his career, and developed a lucrative law practice. By the time of Scopes trial, he charged fees of up of to two hundred thousand dollars per case and was much in demand, even at those prices. The Scopes trial was the only time in his entire professional career that Darrow offered his legal services for free, which demonstrated just how much he opposed anti-evolution laws.

Prosecutor William Jennings Bryan, age sixty-five, posed for this photograph in the courtroom during the Scopes trial. This picture suggests the physical strain on Bryan produced by the oppressive heat in the courtroom, which at time exceeded 100 degrees without any breeze. To counter the heat, Bryan regularly removed his suit jacket, tie, and shirt collar. Since he was overweight, he sweated profusely. Although Bryan had been trained as an attorney, he had not practiced law in over three decades. Instead, he had served in public office and made a comfortable living as a speaker and writer for political and religious causes. Bryan remained a political progressive and a religious conservative throughout his career. By the 1920s, he began seeing belief in the Darwinian theory of human evolution as a root cause of social, moral, and spiritual problems—particularly militarism, the exploitation of labor, and religious indifference. This led Bryan to campaign for laws against the teaching of evolution in public schools. Viewing the trial as a further opportunity to promote this cause, Bryan volunteered his services to defend the Tennessee anti-evolution statute when it was challenged in the Scopes case.

READ
"WHY DAYTON
OF ALL PLACES"

For Sale at
ROBINSON'S DRUG STORE,
On Main Street

Dayton druggist and school board president Fred Robinson (left center, bare-headed) is pictured here selling copies of a local promotional booklet issued by Dayton civic leaders in conjunction with the Scopes trial. The booklet's name, "Why Dayton of All Places," came from the title of a *St. Louis Post-Dispatch* editorial ridiculing the trial's origins and location. The booklet attempted to capitalize on the trial as a means to promote Dayton. It avoided taking sides on the issue of teaching evolution and instead boosted Dayton as a place to live and work. The booklet described both economic opportunities for investors and recreational opportunities for visitors. The trial coincided with an unusually severe heat wave, however, so that instead of promoting Dayton as a place to live and work, the trial mostly burned images of oppressive heat into the public mind. The trial's major legacy to Dayton was the establishment there of a small Christian college as a memorial to William Jennings Bryan.

Local merchants tried to profit from the Scopes trial and the crowds it attracted to Dayton. Stores stocked up on books on both sides of the evolution issue, as well as on items of interest to visitors generally. Advertising tended to link products to the trial in some way, particularly with regard to the Darwinian theory of human evolution. Dayton downtown clothier J. R. Darwin took advantage of his last name to attract customers to his shop with banners and signs. He joked that his clothes were the fittest, a play on the concept of the survival of the fittest underlying Charles Darwin's theory of evolution. He also erected a banner declaring, "DARWIN IS RIGHT inside," with a hand pointing toward his shop. This photograph shows Darwin's Market Street shop during the Scopes trial with a banner advertising "DARWIN'S BIG SALE."

On his own initiative, San Francisco rabbi Herman Rosennasser (standing, third from the left) went to Dayton during the Scopes trial to assist the defense in challenging the anti-evolution statute. He so impressed defense lawyers with his knowledge of the Hebrew scriptures, which included the Genesis account of creation at issue in the trial, that they invited him to serve as an expert witness on interpreting the Bible. In this photograph, Rosennasser delivers a mock class in biblical translation staged by the defense for the media and curious visitors. Members of the defense team stand to the right of the Hebrew script (from left to right), New York attorney Arthur Garfield Hays, Knoxville attorney John R. Neal, defendant John Scopes, and New York attorney Dudley Field Malone. Local trial instigator George Rappleyea stands with his arm around Rosennasser. Assorted reporters stand around Rappleyea and Rosennasser.

This photograph captures a typical scene along Market Street in downtown Dayton during the Scopes trial. Hundreds of local citizens and out-of-town visitors, dressed-up somewhat for the event despite the heat, watched the passing scene as Bryan, Darrow, and other famous litigators walked to and from the courthouse. The street itself became alive with carnival games and booths selling refreshments and souvenirs. It had all the trappings of a downtown fair and attracted people from the surrounding countryside to see what all the excitement was about, even if they could not obtain a seat in the overcrowded courtroom. For many, events outside proved more entertaining than the actual trial anyway—and not so uncomfortably hot. Although Dayton civic leaders originally expected thousands of trial spectators from all over the country, few people other than trial participants and representatives of the media came from very far away. Most of the spectators, like those shown in this photograph, hailed from Dayton or from the immediately surrounding countryside.

Crowds formed rapidly along Market Street in Dayton during the Scopes trial. People milled about, watching and waiting as events unfolded. Robinson's Drug Store, standing nearly across the street from the Rhea County Courthouse and offering a popular soda fountain and newsstand, became a favorite place for visitors and local people to congregate. This photograph shows a mixed assembly of townspeople and farmers, men and women, and adults and children, crowding around the drugstore entrance—a sure sign that some trial notable was standing near the door.

The Scopes trial began with jury selection, which was conducted on the first day of the trial—Friday, July 10, 1925. Many trial observers had predicted that the attorneys would take several days to select suitable jurors for the controversial case, especially if defense counsel Clarence Darrow held out for ones that might be willing to acquit his client. Darrow had a different legal strategy in mind, however. He wanted to convict the statute in the public mind rather than acquit his client of a minor offense that carried no threat of imprisonment. The defense objected to the very idea that the people, acting through a legislature or a jury, should stand in judgment of a scientific theory, such as the theory of evolution. For this, Darrow did not need or want sophisticated jurors who could understand science, religion, or arguments for and against teaching evolution. He quickly accepted almost everyone called to serve on the jury, including one illiterate farmer. Only one juror came from Dayton; all the others lived in rural Rhea County. The entire jury-selection process took a few hours, rather than days, permitting the court to adjourn early for the weekend. This photograph shows jurors being sworn in by the court.

The Scopes trial was conducted in a mammoth court-room on the second floor of the Rhea County Court-house in Dayton. The courtroom had large windows on three sides, but no ceiling fans to circulate the air on still days. It was the largest trial courtroom in Tennessee, with seats for over five hundred persons and standing room for hundreds more. This photograph was taken during the Scopes trial from the front of the courtroom next to the judge's bench, the edge of which appears in the picture's lower right corner. Every seat is taken and people are standing in the rear of the courtroom. Jurors sit in the center of this picture, directly facing the bench. The attorneys sit at the long, rectangular opposing tables on the right and left sides of the photograph. A table for four stenographers transcribing the proceedings sits directly in the middle between the lawyers, judge, and jury. A rail, visible between the jurors and behind the lawyer's table at right, divides this raised central part of the courtroom from the crowd of spectators and reporters.

At the Scopes trial, prosecutors and defense attorneys had to fight for space in the crush of spectators and reporters. At times, the lawyers had to stand in order to see what was happening in the trial, as in this photograph of several attorneys watching Clarence Darrow apologize to the court for contemptuous remarks he had made earlier in the proceedings. The court had ordered Darrow to show cause why he should not be held in contempt for suggesting that his client could not get a fair trial. Darrow's apology to the court, followed by the judge's dismissal of the contempt proceedings, represented one of the most dramatic moments of the trial. Here, to the right of the microphone, stand from left to right local prosecutors J. Gordon McKenzie, Wallace Haggard, Herbert Hicks, and Tom Stewart, listening intently. Standing to the left of the microphone is New York defense counsel and longtime Darrow friend Dudley Field Malone. One of three courtroom microphones from pioneer radio station WGN appears in the foreground, on the post. The Chicago station broadcast the entire trial to listeners throughout the Midwest.

When the Scopes trial began, local men eagerly sought places on the jury, expecting that jurors would have front-row seats in the crowded courtroom. As it turned out, jurors missed most of the proceedings because the two most hotly contested issues—the validity of the anti-evolution statute and the admissibility of expert testimony—involved issues of law decided by the court rather than issues of fact for the jury. Following customary practice, the court excused jurors while the lawyers debated these two legal issues, which generated the most stirring oratory of the entire trial. This photograph captures one of those moments, with the front-row jury seats empty, when defense lawyer Clarence Darrow (left center, facing camera) crossed over to the prosecution table to talk with William Jennings Bryan (left center, leaning over table). The other prosecutors flank Bryan at the table. Under American trial practice, the jury's role involves finding the facts of the case and applying those facts to the given law. Neither of these were much disputed in the Scopes trial. A newsreel camera stands in the far right corner of the courtroom, recording the entire scene, while a news photographer in the center of this picture takes a still photo of Bryan and Darrow.

With the jury back in the courtroom, Darrow, in shirt sleeves and suspenders, argues his client's case to the Scopes trial jurors, all of whom wear coats and ties in this photograph. The attorneys, in contrast, typically removed their coats during the proceedings. The back of the head of defense attorney Dudley Field Malone appears in the lower left corner, next to a radio microphone. Even though women had gained the right to vote throughout the United States in 1920 and generally served on juries in Tennessee at the time of the Scopes trial, the local custom in Dayton precluded their service as jurors and discouraged their attendance at court proceedings. All of the jurors, court personnel, and attorneys for the Scopes trial, and most of the spectators and reporters in the courtroom, were men.

William Jennings Bryan, in shirt sleeves and wearing a bow tie, stands to engage in a legal argument during the Scopes trial. His reading glasses hang from his pocket. Local prosecutor Ben McKenzie, who had served as state's attorney for Dayton before his retirement, sits with his arms folded next to Bryan. Ben McKenzie's son Gordon, also a local attorney serving with the prosecution team, sits at the extreme right, looking left. Five Dayton attorneys joined state's attorney Tom Stewart from nearby Winchester, Tennessee, on the prosecution team, which also included Bryan and William Jennings Bryan Jr. The defense team was even larger, featuring several attorneys from New York, Clarence Darrow from Chicago, and various Tennessee attorneys from Knoxville and Nashville. This legal talent, assembled in Dayton for a misdemeanor case, helped transform the Scopes trial into a world famous event. Few legal points went uncontested.

As the centerpiece of their planned legal arguments in the Scopes trial, the defense assembled a team of scientists to testify as expert witnesses about the theory of evolution and the importance of teaching about it as part of the high school biology curriculum. Their testimony was intended to educate the court and the public about the controversial subject. Prosecutors vowed to oppose the introduction of such testimony as irrelevant to the narrow issue of whether John Scopes had violated the law. In this photograph, the assembled scientists posed for the press before the Mansion, a large house in Dayton that served as defense headquarters during the trial. The pictured scientists are (front row from left to right) University of Missouri zoologist Winterton C. Curtis, Tennessee state geologist Wilbur A. Nelson, Southwestern College biologist William M. Goldsmith, (back row from left to right) University of Chicago zoologist Horatio Hackett Newman, Johns Hopkins University zoologist Maynard M. Metcalf, University of Chicago anthropologist Fay Cooper Cole, and New Jersey Agriculture Station director Jacob G. Lipman. Siding with the prosecution, the court barred expert testimony about evolution, precluding testimony from these scientists. Their written depositions were read into the court record for review by the appellate court, however, and these depositions were widely reprinted in newspapers.

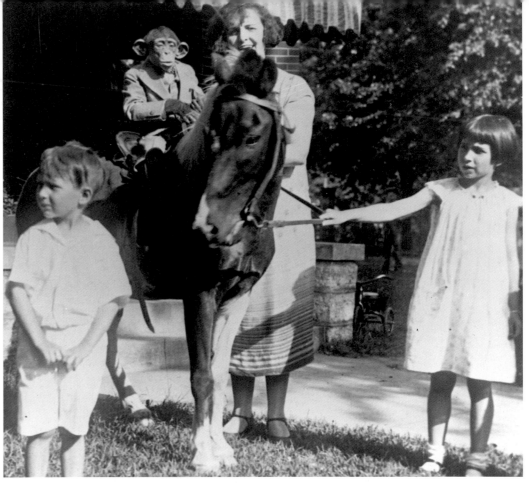

Journalists billed the court proceedings as the "monkey trial" before it even began. The name captured the popular understanding that the principal dispute in the Scopes trial involved whether humans evolved from monkeys. As part of the carnival atmosphere surrounding the Scopes trial, hucksters brought monkeys and chimpanzees to Dayton, where they posed with townspeople and visitors for a fee. Dayton druggist Fred Robinson, one of the most enterprising of the local business owners, arranged for a monkey to greet customers at his downtown store. Robinson's monkey was named Joe Mendi. He wore a plaid suit with bow tie to emphasize the link to humans, and entertained people with his human-like antics. In these photographs with the Robinson family, the monkey is shown riding a horse at Robinson's house, drinking a soda at Robinson's drug store, and playing a toy piano for Robinson's children and their friends. It was all part of the fun at Dayton.

Dayton shopkeepers sold various monkey-related souvenirs to visitors and townspeople during the Scopes trial. Among the most popular of these trial souvenirs were stuffed toy monkeys. Fred Robinson carried a full line of such souvenirs at his downtown drugstore, where the proceedings against John Scopes had begun. This photograph shows Robinson family and friends with stuffed toy monkeys. Other shops offered monkey canes and carved wooden monkeys. The town minted a special souvenir coin featuring the head of a monkey wearing a stylish straw hat. Robinson's drugstore offered special "simian sodas" as a fountain drink. For a while, one Dayton constable put a sign reading "Monkeyville Police" on his official motorcycle. Townspeople could hardly object when the national press designated the proceedings as the "monkey trial," yet many did.

Anticipating more visitors for the trial than could fit into the courtroom, Rhea County officials installed benches and an outdoor speaker system on the spacious courthouse lawn to serve as overflow seating. They also erected a platform on the lawn for evening entertainment. Local townspeople hung a banner on the courthouse wall, admonishing spectators to "Read Your BIBLE." These outdoor facilities became the setting for the trial's most famous event. After cracks appeared in the ceiling beneath the courthouse's packed second-floor courtroom, the judge moved the proceedings outside. This occurred during the afternoon of July 20, 1925, when the trial appeared all but over except for closing arguments by Clarence Darrow and William Jennings Bryan. Moving the proceedings outside had the further advantage of permitting many more spectators to witness those much-awaited closing arguments. Instead of closing, however, the defense called Bryan to the stand as an expert on the Bible. Bryan accepted the offer over the objections of the other prosecutors. Darrow grilled Bryan on biblical literalism for over two hours, exposing the fundamentalist cause to public ridicule in the national media. It ended the otherwise successful prosecution of John Scopes on a sour note for Bryan.

Perhaps no physical artifact is more closely associated with the Scopes trial in the public mind than the palm-leaf fan. Local businesses distributed them as advertising devices, including the one here held by William Jennings Bryan. It bears a commercial advertisement for Fred Robinson's drugstore. Participants and spectators used such fans throughout the eight-day trial, as afternoon temperatures soared above 100 degrees inside the courtroom. Although the courtroom had large windows, spectators standing in front of them blocked any possible breeze. Midway through the trial, after several people fainted from heat exhaustion in the courtroom, county officials installed electric ceiling fans. Bryan continued to use a hand fan to supplement the ceiling fans. The physical stress of the heat, coupled with the mental stress of the trial, probably contributed to Bryan's death from apoplexy five days after the trial ended.

The heat impacted everyone at the Scopes trial, but none of the trial participants appeared to suffer more than local prosecutor Ben McKenzie. He fainted from the heat early in the trial and often appeared on the verge of collapse. The oldest attorney on either side, McKenzie had once served as the state's attorney for Dayton's judicial district. Tom Stewart held this position in 1925, and he led the Scopes prosecution. McKenzie volunteered his services for the highly publicized trial, however, and made several minor arguments during the court proceedings. His transparent good nature and flowery, old-fashioned speaking style made him a favorite among attorneys on both sides of the case. When he addressed the court or spoke formally to reporters, he sounded like the stereotype of a nineteenth-century politician. Defense attorneys initially objected to many of McKenzie's comments, but once they grew to know McKenzie and understand his speaking style, friendships developed between the elderly lawyer and opposing counsel. When McKenzie nearly fainted for a second time during the trial, defense attorney Dudley Field Malone rushed to assist him and offered to pay for installing electric ceiling fans in the courtroom.

The subject matter of and publicity generated by the Scopes trial attracted itinerant evangelists to preach in the streets and churches of Dayton. They became part of the spectacle, competing for attention with famous attorneys, circus monkeys, and carnival games. Some of the evangelists came to pray in support of Bryan and the prosecution; others focused on preaching to Scopes and his defenders. Among the most famous of the itinerant evangelists to visit Dayton at this time was T. T. Martin of Blue Mountain, Mississippi. Martin had joined the crusade against evolution two years earlier with a fiery book about the dangers of teaching evolution, entitled *Hell in the High School.* He hawked that book and others from an open-air stand on Market Street in downtown Dayton during each day of trial and preached revival sermons on the courthouse lawn every evening. This photograph shows him attracting a small crowd on the street during one day of the trial.

As expected by many court observers, the jury convicted John Scopes of violating Tennessee's law against teaching evolution. From the outset, the defense focused more on challenging the validity of the statute than on defending Scopes's innocence under it. Indeed, in his final comment to the jury, defense attorney Clarence Darrow urged jurors to convict his client so that the defense could appeal the case to a higher court, which might strike down the anti-evolution statute as unconstitutional. The jury complied after conferring for only a few minutes. This photograph shows Scopes, flanked by the police and his attorneys, standing to hear the jury's verdict. Conviction carried a fine from one hundred to five hundred dollars, which the *Baltimore Sun* offered to pay on Scopes's behalf. When the jury did not set the amount of the fine, Judge John Raulston imposed the minimum amount. In 1927, the Tennessee Supreme Court set aside Scopes's conviction on the grounds that the judge, rather than the jury, fixed the amount of the fine. Defense counsel denounced the appellate court's ruling as a subterfuge to prevent further appeal to the U.S. Supreme Court. The ruling ended the Scopes case, but left Tennessee's anti-evolution statute intact. Prosecutors brought no further indictments under the law, however, and the state legislature repealed it in 1967.

The Scopes trial ended on Tuesday, July 21, 1925, with the conviction of John Scopes. The court's ruling, however, did not end the matter for attorneys on either side. Darrow and the other defense attorneys immediately began planning their appeal of Scopes's conviction. Ever the politician, Bryan set about trying to capitalize on the public interest stirred by the Scopes trial to reinvigorate his crusade against the teaching of human evolution in public schools. He planned a speaking tour to deliver his closing arguments in the Scopes trial to public audiences across the country; he gave the speech once in nearby Winchester, Tennessee, at the invitation of prosecutor Tom Stewart. Bryan remained in Dayton through the weekend to oversee the printing in Chattanooga of his closing arguments as a pamphlet designed for mass distribution. He finished this task on Saturday, July 25, and returned to his temporary residence in Dayton late that evening. Following church service the next day, Bryan died in his sleep during an afternoon nap. Much of the nation mourned the Great Commoner's passing. This photograph shows Bryan's casket being loaded on a special train in Dayton for transport to Washington, D.C. People lined the tracks to watch the train pass on its journey to the nation's capital, and thousands turned out for Bryan's funeral in Arlington National Cemetery. For many of his faithful followers, Bryan became a martyr to the anti-evolution cause, which continued to live on even after Bryan died. Two other states soon passed anti-evolution statutes modeled on the Tennessee law. More recently, some states and localities have sought to balance the teaching of evolution with instruction in creation as Americans continue to debate the issue of human origins.

Afterword: Seventy-five Years of Scopes

On March 28, 1996, John Wilder started talking about God on the floor of the Tennessee State Senate. It was not an unusual topic for the setting—the senate convenes each morning with a prayer—but Wilder's speech was notable. The Democrat from Fayette County, majority leader of the senate, and therefore the de facto lieutenant governor of the state, was trying to explain his opposition to a proposed bill that would have placed restrictions on teaching evolution in Tennessee public schools.

"I know God," Wilder said. "The total God. Today we're talking about God the creator. He's not little. He's big. We're here today because we're confused about how he does things." He went on to say he could not find any conflict between the biblical story of creation and the scientific evidence that all life—including humans—has evolved and changed over time. He cautioned against restrictions on scientific inquiry, reminding his colleagues that in earlier ages scientists had faced prosecution for making heretical assertions that the earth is round. But at the close of his speech, which one newspaper described as a "Roman-like oration," Wilder again stressed his religious devotion: "I can't vote for this," he said. "But I don't want you to think I don't know God."[1]

Wilder carried the day. The bill went down by a twenty to thirteen vote in the senate and never resurfaced. But the caution and the protestations of faith displayed by a man some considered the most powerful politician in

Tennessee at the time were testimony to the symbolic strength the issue still wielded. Evolution remains a delicate subject in many parts of the country, particularly in the "Bible Belt." But its significance is magnified in Tennessee, the most visible, one of the earliest, and—in the public imagination—the most important testing grounds for Darwin's ideas in America.

Seventy-five years after the Scopes trial, the state that hosted the great courtroom debate still bears the trial's scars—albeit perhaps not in expected or obvious ways. The trial's legacy in the Volunteer State is complicated and contradictory. Because of the way the "monkey trial" was framed in the national and international media—both at the time and even more so in subsequent years—the issues it raised continue to provoke an odd mixture of embarrassment and defiance among Tennesseans. It is possible, in fact, to see Tennessee itself as the only real loser in the Scopes Trial. While the ideological parties involved both gained something from the case—the ACLU and its supporters took a step toward bolstering individual rights; the fundamentalists acquired a martyr, William Jennings Bryan, and a unifying cause—the state that had politely if naively set the stage for the whole affair earned nothing but lasting public ridicule. Tennessee, arguably the least "southern" of the southern states, a state that had strongly divided loyalties during the Civil War, became for some a symbol of backward, southern small-mindedness. (It is interesting that East Tennessee, home of the Scopes trial, had been largely pro-Union during the Civil War and remained steadfastly Republican even after the Reconstruction. Yet this region, with its Appalachian roots and bedrock Baptism, has come to be seen—and to see itself—as a bulwark of the South. More than one observer has noted there are more Confederate flags on display now in East Tennessee than there were during the Civil War.) It has given Tennesseans a complex of sorts, one that becomes apparent whenever the question of evolution or religion in the schools arises in public debate. On the one hand, there's a desire to distance the state from the trial and everything that went with it. On the other hand, there's a knee-jerk tendency to identify with Bryan and his cause, out of regional pride and enduring religious conviction.

This uneasy balance can be seen in three key areas of Tennessee life and culture: politics, education, and religion. It's clear that the forces that led to the Scopes trial are still present in the state—and that the memory of the trial itself has helped keep them active.

RELIGION: THE GREAT DIVIDE

On a hill just outside of downtown Dayton, Tennessee, there is a cluster of handsome brick buildings that look across the town to slopes and valleys in the distance. A sign at the foot of the hill reads, "Bryan College. Christ Above All." Originally christened William Jennings Bryan University when it opened its doors in 1930, this picturesque campus is one of the most concrete legacies of the Scopes trial in Tennessee. It is also representative in many ways of the impact that case had on Christian fundamentalists here and across the South.

To get at the roots of anti-Darwinism in the state that would come to symbolize it, one must first consider Tennessee's strong and distinctive religious history. The state's prevailing strains of Protestantism have always had a defiant and individualistic nature that trace directly to their pioneer roots. The first ministers in Tennessee were Presbyterian, drawn to the region in the 1770s by the large Scotch-Irish population that had migrated over the mountains from North Carolina. But while they met with some success in winning converts among the scattered and often lawless settlers, the relatively sophisticated and hierarchical denomination was not the one best suited to the tenor of the territory. Samuel Doak, Tennessee's first full-time pastor, was a classically educated Virginian who had earned a baccalaureate degree from Princeton in 1775. Licensed as a minister by Hanover Presbytery, he worked tirelessly to establish congregations in Tennessee—but that was not all. He and his followers also preached the importance of education, a mainstay of Presbyterianism, but not a major cause of concern for the early communities of rural, agricultural Tennessee. Nevertheless, Presbyterians managed to establish several academic institutions. Some of them, including Tusculum College in Greeneville and Maryville College in Blount County, survive today, albeit in different form.[2]

At about the same time, the first Baptist congregations were taking shape in Tennessee. Unlike the Presbyterians, they tended to be organized not by visiting evangelists but from the ground up by settlers who had moved from Virginia and North Carolina. The Baptists usually appointed their own pastor from among the congregation; "ordination" was awarded by a vote of the church membership. Pastors almost always had full-time occupations—they included farmers, blacksmiths, etc.—and received no money for their ministerial service. It was a system of strict self-reliance perfectly matched to the geographic isolation and temperament of the state's early communities. Not surprisingly for a denomination rooted in simple adherence to biblical principles, Baptists had little use for formal, "worldly" education. Among the most strident opponents of academic pursuits was the faction that came to be known as Primitive Baptists, who opposed even missionary work.[3]

The other major religious force in the state is the Methodist Church, which came to prominence in the early 1800s during that century's first Great Revival. Methodist "circuit riders," ministers who rode on horseback between many communities, were omnipresent and aggressive in recruiting church members. One frontier proverb remarked on their persistence in fair or foul weather: "There is nothing out today but crows and Methodist preachers."[4] Less doctrinally severe than the Baptists but more fiery and populist in approach than the stern Presbyterians, the Methodists helped establish multiple-day revivals and camp meetings as major components of Tennessee religious life. Baptist groups quickly appropriated the same tools, and both Baptists and Methodists gained converts, while Presbyterians waned significantly.

As the state matured, all of its denominations began to look for ways to consolidate and better purvey their evangelism. One significant outreach effort was the establishment of educational facilities. Following the lead of the Presbyterians, the state's religious associations began in the 1830s to open schools and colleges across Tennessee. But the slowest to act were the Baptists, particularly the Primitive faction, which was torn between suspicion of secularism and a desire not to lose membership among their wealthier, better-educated congregants. Baptist schools were eventually founded in the 1840s and 1850s, but the debate over the dangers of education never entirely subsided.[5]

Almost all of Tennessee's denominations were splintered by the issue of slavery and the subsequent Civil War, with both Baptists and Methodists splitting along regional lines. The Southern Baptist Convention formed in the 1840s as a reaction against northern Baptist abolitionism. The stance was in keeping with Baptists' emphasis on self-sufficiency and resistance to hierarchical dictates. After the war, the southern denominations, like the South itself, had to rebuild. They were aided by another religious "reawakening," which the war's disruption of normal religious life helped produce. The resultant swelling of congregations reaffirmed the Baptist and Methodist predominance in Tennessee, with Baptists emerging as the largest denomination in the state.[6] The inward-directed faith both denominations embraced appealed to a demoralized population that had been branded as the enemy by the rest of the nation. As Herman A. Norton puts it in *Religion in Tennessee, 1777–1945:*

The evangelical Protestantism—reaching out almost exclusively to the salvation of souls, with ministry understood individualistically— that was reforged by competitive evangelism and regular congregational preaching, in the sectarian atmosphere of this period, set the pattern for religious activity in Tennessee for the remainder of the century, and for much of the next. With little sense of remorse for past evils and virtually devoid of social ethics, this type of religion was destined to be defensive of regional mores as it urged the self-conscious society to turn in upon itself. Playing a major role in conserving "the old ways," evangelical Protestantism became a powerful force and made a near conquest of the state's population.[7]

This regional defensiveness and mistrust of modern, imported ideas were major factors in bringing the evolution controversy to Tennessee. But it was a controversy that built slowly.

The homogeneity, not to say hegemony, of Protestantism in the state insulated it in some ways from the debates that were beginning elsewhere in the country. With the rise of industrialization and unionization, the Northeast and Midwest in the late nineteenth century saw the emergence of the "Social Gospel" movement, concerned with using Christian teachings to advocate for social reform. Meanwhile, some liberal Protestants had begun to rethink the Bible itself, reinterpreting it in light of new historical and scientific thought. Part of that thought, of course, was Darwinism. But even as an inevitable reaction started among conservatives to the liberal theologians—most notably with "The Fundamentals," a series of essays published at the beginning of the twentieth century that helped set the foundation for fundamentalism—evolution was not necessarily seen as anathema. Instead, even evangelical writers looked for ways to incorporate some form of evolutionary thinking, albeit always in an explicitly creator-driven framework.[8] This general, sometimes grudging tolerance of Darwin's ideas led to widespread dissemination of them, most notably in increasingly sophisticated school science texts.

Schoolbooks had not ignored Darwin in the nineteenth century, but they had begun from an assumption of intelligent creation, seeing evolution as a tool of the creator rather than a challenge to creationism itself. In the new century of electricity and flight and mass industry, however, a more thoroughly scientific viewpoint came into instructional vogue. By the end of World War I, textbooks were routinely describing Darwin as the father of modern, rational scientific thought.[9] Those texts reached even states such as Tennessee, where the clash between modernism and traditionalism had yet to gain much force simply because modernism had very little presence.

By the 1920s, even the relatively isolated communities of the South began to feel the impact of new technologies and new ideas, many of which—motion pictures, recorded music, etc.—arose from views of the world that were far from biblical. The stage was effectively set so that when fundamentalist leaders, William Jennings Bryan in particular, began to blame Darwin's "survival of the fittest" credo for encouraging violence, godlessness, and a breakdown of the social order, such condemnation struck a chord in Tennessee. Here were ideas imported from a foreign place, academic and European ideas, apparently in direct contradiction of biblical teachings—and they were being taught in every large and small schoolhouse in the state. It's hardly surprising that when Bryan challenged legislatures to take up the issue, many in the South responded. And it's even less surprising that John Washington Butler, the man who finally brought an anti-evolution bill to the floor of the Tennessee House of Representatives, was a devout member of a Primitive Baptist church. (However, it's worth noting that the original impetus for anti-evolution bills came not from Tennessee but from Kentucky, where the Baptist State Board of Missions passed a resolution in 1921 calling for a ban on teaching evolution. That resolution inspired Bryan's own crusade.)[10] What Butler, Bryan, and their supporters could never have imagined was how much the bill would ultimately separate them from much of American society.

Before the Scopes case, fundamentalist Christians had little reason to feel embattled in the South. The Butler Act itself was a good example of the clout religion wielded. But the trial and the publicity that accompanied it helped start a reconfiguration. Commentary on the trial, both national and within the state, drew a thick line between fundamentalists and the modern world. Although no clear victor emerged from the trial, the terms had been defined in such a way that it was clear there

was little room for biblical literalism in the emerging mass culture. Stung by national ridicule and sensing that the rest of the nation was headed toward a secular, materialist epoch, fundamentalist churches began to pull back from involvement in the national mainstream. Although Christian forces remained active enough to lobby for a spate of anti-evolution bills in other southern states just after the Scopes case, religious interest in such public affairs became increasingly rare. As Joel A. Carpenter puts it in *Revive Us Again*, his study of fundamentalism in the 1930s and 1940s, "fundamentalists were becoming a distinct religious community by the early 1930s. By that time it had become clear to many fundamentalists that their ability to gain a respectful hearing in Protestant forums or in the more secular community was coming to an end."[11] Instead, fundamentalists in Tennessee and elsewhere engaged in a kind of separatism, developing more and more of their own schools, media, and other institutions. A significant example was Bryan College.

During the Scopes trial, Dayton School Superintendent Walter White had suggested creating a Bible-oriented school in Dayton and naming it after Bryan. This prompted a ten-thousand-dollar pledge from Florida philanthropist George F. Washburn, who wrote to White, "This fight in Dayton is 'the beginning of the battle that will encircle the world.' This is a psychological moment to establish a Fundamentalist university."[12] After Bryan's martyr-like death, the school assumed the status of a memorial to the most popular fundamentalist leader of the day. And the men who ran Bryan College never forgot the cause that had brought their namesake to Dayton. Anti-evolutionist speakers were regular visitors from the 1930s on.[13] But even this institution, named for one of the most public figures in American life, rarely engaged in any sort of activity beyond its own walls. The few exceptions, significantly, were during early attempts to repeal the Butler Act. In 1935 and again in 1952, Tennessee legislators unsuccessfully proposed overturning the old "monkey law." Both times, the leading opposition came in letters and petitions from students and faculty at Bryan College.[14]

Anti-evolutionism was hardly dead, however. Even as the Scopes case became enshrined by the secular culture (however in-accurately) as a victory of reason over narrow-minded dogma, it assumed an entirely different meaning for fundamentalists. It was the challenge they had not backed away from, and the scorn that resulted only served to strengthen their opposition to Darwinian thought. Interestingly, Tennessee's growth as a center of scientific innovation in the wake of the Great Depression and World War II—particularly with the creation of the Tennessee Valley Authority and in Oak Ridge—came in the region of the state most closely identified with old-line religion and had seemingly little effect on fundamentalist doctrine.

As will be seen, the fundamentalist withdrawal from secular life coincided with an era of general caution about evolution in the educational arena. If Tennessee's conservative Christians were not publicly fighting evolution in the classroom, it was at least partly because there was not much there to fight. (At least, as they understood it. When writer Orland Kay Armstrong toured Tennessee in 1929 to assess the impact of the Scopes case and the Butler Act, he found teachers and professors incorporating Darwinian concepts in disguise, often using words like "development" in place of "evolution." One academic told Armstrong, "We are not going to teach a 17th century science because of a 17th century law! We are simply making an effort to be inoffensive to the existing law in our promulgation of truth!")[15]

Meanwhile, the Scopes trial was followed by several decades of increasingly sophisticated attempts to devise a biblically-derived account of the earth's origins that would square with the biological and geological records. The field that emerged, which came to be known as "creation science," itself evolved over the years from simply looking for holes in mainstream Darwinistic thought to a progressively complex set of assumptions involving a "young earth" (less than ten thousand years old) and relying on the biblical story of Noah's flood to account for most modern geological features. As early as 1923, during Bryan's campaign for anti-evolution laws, creationist and self-styled geologist George McReady Price published a 726-page textbook called *The New Geology*, a Genesis-based book that inspired generations of creationists.[16]

Creationists were largely quiet during the post-Scopes lull, displaced even among evangelicals by more conciliatory groups like the American Scientific Affiliation, a Christian group that was careful to avoid direct confrontation with evolutionists. But the uneasy truce could last only as long as neither side pushed its case too strenuously. And in the late 1950s and early 1960s, with a new push for science education in the wake of the Sputnik launch, evolution made a strong reappearance in public school textbooks. Just as the Scopes case had prompted fundamentalists to distance themselves from mainstream culture, the renewed emphasis on evolution helped trigger their re-engagement. They had been building back toward a public presence for more than a decade, behind the leadership of a new set of popular evangelists, most notably Billy Graham. Now, as science historian Ronald L. Numbers puts it, "All of a sudden, you had hundreds of thousands of young people coming home from school telling their parents what they were learning."[17] This happened within a few years of the U.S. Supreme Court's banning of organized prayer from public schools. A new wave of fundamentalist activism began, led by groups such as Phyllis Schlafly's Eagle Forum.

Among the new activity was a renewed emphasis on creation science. The most significant development was the founding of the Creation Research Society in 1963, which pulled together a small group of creationists with varying degrees of scientific background to form a unified anti-evolution front. Based in St. Joseph, Missouri, the group expanded within its first decade to about 2,000 members, including 412 credentialed scientists.[18] CRS operated on several fronts, publishing a creation-based school textbook which it encouraged states to offer as an alternative in their public schools (Tennessee, as will be seen, was one of the first states to pass "equal time" legislation allowing creation science in the classroom), organizing debates on college campuses, and funding research efforts to find geological or biological evidence of the events described in Genesis. These efforts continue today, although CRS has been joined in the field by a host of similar and/or splinter organizations, including the large California-based Institute for Creation Research.

While none of these groups is based in Tennessee, the state has been home to a handful of significant creation scientists and gatherings. Among the most interesting figures in the "creation science" field over the past three decades has been a maverick scientist named Robert Gentry, who lives in the community of Powell just outside Knoxville. A trained physicist, Gentry managed to obtain a "visiting scientist" position in the late 1960s at none other than Oak Ridge National Laboratory (ORNL), arguably Tennessee's premier scientific research center. Gentry's work with "superheavy" elements piqued the interest of nuclear researchers there during the Cold War. Whatever the significance of his findings from a national defense standpoint, however, they were actually a byproduct of his efforts to find evidence of biblical creation. A Seventh-Day Adventist, Gentry has published books and produced videos arguing that a phenomenon known as pleochroic halos—microscopic concentric ring patterns formed in some granites by the rapid decay of radioactive elements—do not conform to conventional views of elemental decay and of the age of the earth. These contentions marginalized him in the world of mainstream science, but he has nevertheless published articles in both *Nature* and *Science,* two of the leading international scientific journals. When he testified in favor of creation science during a 1981 anti-evolution case in Arkansas, he found his position at ORNL terminated soon afterward. His work has continued unabated in the years since, with funding coming entirely from donations. Most recently, he has turned his attention to cosmology and astronomy, attempting to prove mathematically that the earth may actually be at or near the center of the universe.

An even more prominent role has been played in recent years by Bryan College. Partly in response to pro-evolution "Darwin Day" events at the University of Tennessee, which will be discussed later, the college in 1998 hosted an "Origins Conference," which drew creationists from around the country to two days of seminars and panel discussions. The significance of such an event at a school named for Bryan, just a few miles from the courthouse where he argued his case, was not lost on the attendees. School officials said they planned more such conferences in the future. In the meantime, some of the leading work in current creation science is being conducted on the Bryan College campus, by one

of the most formidably credentialed researchers in the creationist camp.

Kurt Wise came to Bryan College after earning a Ph.D. in paleontology from Harvard University. At Harvard, he studied under Steven Jay Gould, a popular biology writer and an avowed evolutionist. But Wise, who grew up in a strongly Baptist family in rural Illinois, emerged from the program with his belief in the biblical creation story unshaken. A serious scientist, he has raised the ire of many creationists by dismissing much existing creation science as poorly researched and reasoned. Calling evolution "a very good theory," he has set out to devise one that can stand up to it scientifically and also match the sequence of creation events described in Genesis. With an international network of geologists, astronomers, and biologists, he hopes to present a unified creation model that will shake evolution's hold on the science establishment. "It'll be years before I'm satisfied enough with a model to toss it out into the scientific community," he has said. "But I'm working on that."[19] If and when he does, it will again put Dayton, Tennessee, at the center of evolution/creation debates.

For now, the issue remains very much alive in Tennessee churches. Many Baptist and Methodist congregations regularly schedule visits by touring lecturers who assail Darwinism and neo-Darwinism with the same intensity William Jennings Bryan did in the 1920s. And few of them fail to invoke Bryan's name and legacy in urging Tennesseans to keep the fight alive. In parts of the religious realm, at least, the Scopes case remains a benchmark for keeping the faith.

POLITICS: THE PRAGMATISTS?

One of the great but least remarked ironies of the Scopes trial is that the Butler Act—which for many in Tennessee came to symbolize the worst kind of reactionary anti-intellectualism—became law just a few days before the Tennessee legislature passed a comprehensive Education Reform Act. The education bill was the project of Gov. Austin Peay, who, like many other governors of the 1920s, saw a need to standardize public schooling in the state and provide resources for more and better teachers. The General Education Law of 1925, which created the state Board of Education and set guidelines for local school systems, remains the basis of Tennessee public education. Other states, including Mississippi and Michigan, used it as a model for their own school legislation.[20] The General Education Law did not pass the legislature easily, surviving 156 proposed amendments and several days of argument. That Peay could simultaneously support an ambitiously progressive education plan and not oppose the Butler Act illustrates the complex political realities of the evolution debate in Tennessee—realities that persist to this day, but in a considerably modified form.

Peay's election to the governorship in 1922 was itself a remarkable turning point in Tennessee politics. A no-nonsense Democrat who ran on a nuts-and-bolts platform of making state government more efficient and effective, he was almost the exact opposite in style and substance of the Republican incumbent, Alf Taylor. On the stump, Taylor told homilies about his dog, "Old Limber"; Peay talked about building highways and lowering taxes.[21] Peay's strongest support in his first campaign came from progressive civic and business leaders, particularly in the state's urban areas.

But after his election, those supporters became disenchanted when Peay pushed forward aggressive reforms that tended to tax the more prosperous areas to fund improvements in rural counties. For example, he reduced the statewide property tax, a move that especially helped farmers, and made up for the lost revenue by an increase in the excise tax on corporate profits. Although he made good on his promise to streamline state government, consolidating its mushrooming bureaucracies into eight departments, he found himself increasingly forced to turn to the rural counties for the legislative support he needed.[22]

By 1925, Peay was in his second two-year term. (He was elected again in 1926, but died in 1927 before completing his third term.) Having focused on administrative overhauls and highway programs in his first two years, he now turned his attention to the state's schools. His education reform bill, which was mostly drawn up by Peay's appointed education commissioner, Perry L. Harned, guaranteed sufficient state funding for all counties to keep schools in session eight months a year. It also established a state salary schedule for teachers and standardized teacher-licensing requirements. To fund the program, Peay proposed a controversial 10 percent tax on tobacco, a measure that would win him no friends in agricultural counties.

It is not surprising, then, that Peay (who was later dubbed "The Maker of Modern Tennessee") was not inclined politically to fight the Butler Act. The anti-evolution bill had its strongest resonance in precisely the areas of the state where Peay needed the most support. There are probably two other reasons for his tacit acceptance of a bill that even at the time Tennessee newspaper editorialists were calling "a jackass measure."[23] The first was personal and undoubtedly sincere. Peay was a lifelong Baptist who had once warned Tennessee college students (long before he himself had a state university named in his honor), "Be loyal to your religion; scientists and cranks will seek to better it. The Christian faith of our people is the bedrock of our institutions."[24] He was wary of teachers with anti-religion agendas bringing "so-called science" into classrooms to undermine their students' faith. Moreover, focused as he was on his own legislative agenda, Peay simply did not consider the Butler Act a significant issue. There is every indication that the governor, like many of the legislators who supported it, saw the measure as a largely symbolic gesture. As Peay understood it, the bill merely blocked schools from assaulting the Bible, which he could not believe would interfere with a reasonable education. Prayer and Bible instruction were still commonplace in schools of the day, so it was not as if the Butler Act was introducing new concepts into the educational arena. At the time, Peay wrote off-handedly, "Nobody believes that it is going to be an active statute."[25]

Peay's attempt at pragmatism turned out to be anything but. However progressive his educational program may have been, it was arguably obscured by the international spectacle that the Butler Act gave rise to in Dayton. Later generations of Tennessee politicians have grappled with the same forces that compelled Peay to support the bill in 1925, with mixed results. There is no question that the long shadow of the Scopes trial, hovering persistently in the wings of the state capitol, has shaped subsequent political dialogue on issues of religion. However, Tennessee's most

recent experience with the evolution controversy suggests that the political calculus has shifted since Peay's day.

John Scopes was the only teacher ever charged under the Butler Act. After Scopes's conviction was thrown out—in a decision that made it clear the state supreme court did not want to have to hear about the act again—the law stayed on the books but reverted more or less to the symbolic status many had envisioned for it in the first place: a statement of faith, rather than practice. Tennessee politicians were neither eager to remind anyone about it nor to raise alarms among their constituents by repealing it. That balance became harder to maintain by the 1960s, however. The decade opened with the film version of *Inherit the Wind,* a hit Broadway play (really a veiled attack on McCarthyism) that presented the Scopes case as a drastically simplified conflict between a dutiful teacher and a town full of bigots. The play and film intensified the image of the South—and Tennessee in particular—as a bastion of small-minded, backwards intolerance. That the script severely distorted history to make its points did not lessen its impact. In the midst of the civil rights movement, it was not hard to believe any depictions of southern bigotry. The people who fought against evolution seemed like clear spiritual ancestors of those who fought for segregation.

Then, in 1967, a Tennessee teacher named Gary L. Scott threatened to take the Butler Act to court after he allegedly lost his temporary teaching post for casting doubt on the literal truth of the Bible in class. A similar case was brewing in Arkansas, and the national media took to calling both of them "Scopes II."[26] The prospect of another "monkey trial" did not appeal to state leaders, especially after a Memphis newspaper, the *Press-Scimitar,* started campaigning vigorously for the Butler Act's repeal. But the law did not go quietly. Even with the attention of the national press once again focused on them, several legislators steadfastly stuck to their mantra of state's rights, local control of education, and, of course, the preeminence of biblical teaching. Still, just a few months after the Scott case arose, in early 1967, both the state house and senate voted to repeal the act. (The Arkansas case, in contrast, proceeded, with that state's supreme court upholding an anti-evolution law. The ACLU promised to appeal to the U.S. Supreme Court, prompting an Arkansas newspaper editorialist to lament, "The fact that the appeal now will have to be carried forward from Arkansas—rather than from Tennessee where the nonsense all started—will be readily productive of the kind of headlines that almost everybody in Arkansas seems to deplore."[27] That anti-evolutionism had neither "started" in nor even centered on Tennessee was a fact long obscured by the enduring symbolism of the Scopes case.)

Still, for a segment of the Tennessee population, anti-evolutionism remained an article of faith and even of cultural pride. The Butler repeal only fueled resentment among religious conservatives, who remained a powerful constituency in many areas of the state. So it was only six years later that a bill with the innocuous title, "An act to amend Tennessee Code Annotated, Section 49-2008, relative to selection of textbooks," resurrected the Butler Act, with a twist. Instead of banning the teaching of evolution, it required science textbooks adopted by the state to also include "other theories, including but not limited to the Genesis account in the Bible." It was the first of what came to be known as "equal time" laws, and similar bills were proposed in several other states over the next few years. (One amendment to the act hastened to add, "The teaching of all occult or satanical beliefs of human origin is expressly excluded from this act," although it offered no definition of "occult.") One of the bill's sponsors in the house was Speaker Ned McWherter, the powerful Democrat who went on to become governor of Tennessee from 1986 to 1994. But the bill really originated with a biology professor named Russell Artist, who taught at David Lipscomb College, a small religious school in Nashville. Artist, a member of the Creation Research Society, had co-written a creationist textbook that had been blocked from the state's public schools by the Tennessee State Textbook Commission (albeit on a technicality).[28] So he turned to the legislature for support, and he found it.

The bill passed the senate easily with no public discussion and passed with minimal debate in the house, on a vote of sixty-nine to sixteen. Not surprisingly, those who voted against it felt compelled to offer explanations.

Rep. Herbert Denton Jr. read into the record: "I opposed House Bill 597, Senate Bill 394, dealing with the teaching of the different accounts of the creation of man for two reasons. I do not feel that the Genesis account of man's creation should be treated as a theory when I accept it as fact, and I feel it could do great harm to any child to be taught the Genesis account of man's creation by a person who could be a non-believer."[29]

A more entertaining objection was offered by Rep. Ben Longley, who also voted no: "Mr. Speaker, with every respect for the intent and purpose of Senate Bill 394, I have asked the sponsor of this bill if it would be possible for a group of draft evaders who fled this country during its hour of need to engage in a marijuana smoking party, to advance a theory of the origin of man and whether this bill would require its teaching to the school children of this state. The sponsor replied that while he did not think it probable, that such was possible."[30]

Nevertheless, on April 30, 1973, the bill became law (only by default, however; Republican governor Winfield Dunn, in a nod to the issue's political delicacy, declined to either sign or veto it). It quickly drew challenges in both state and federal court from groups including the National Association of Biology Teachers and Americans United for Separation of Church and State. The Federal Court of Appeals for the Sixth Circuit settled the issue decisively two years later, throwing the bill out as "patently unconstitutional." In the opinion, Circuit Court Judge George Edwards noted that the intent to displace evolution with biblical teachings "is as clear in the 1973 statute as it was in the statute of 1925. For a state to seek to enforce such a preference by law is to seek to accomplish the very establishment of religion which the First Amendment to the United States Constitution squarely forbids."[31] (Bills in other states reached a similar end, with the most visible being the 1981 Arkansas case that featured testimony from Tennessee creation scientist Robert Gentry.)

In all likelihood, most of those who voted for the 1973 bill saw it much as Austin Peay had seen the Butler Act—a political gesture to assuage a particular constituency that was not intended to have literal consequences. The national media followed the case, but with little of the fanfare given to the Scopes trial—or, indeed, to the Butler Act's repeal. In the era of Vietnam, Watergate, and the energy crisis, anti-evolutionism probably seemed to many in other parts of the country like a curio from a different era.

Although the 1980s began with President Ronald Reagan advocating the inclusion of creation science in classrooms, the decade saw anti-evolution efforts thrown out by courts in several states, culminating in a 1987 U.S. Supreme Court ruling that found a Louisiana "Creationism Act" unconstitutional, on the grounds that "creationism" was a religious doctrine and not a science. In this atmosphere, Tennessee politicians were not eager to push the issue. The sole attempt to resurrect it in that era came from Rep. Pete Drew of Knoxville, who proposed another set of requirements for textbooks, mostly dealing with specific "scientific" objections to evolutionary theory. Much of the language—for example, that the Big Bang theory "is deficient in addressing or accounting for the retrograde axial rotation of Uranus and Venus as well as various satellites and moons of Uranus, Jupiter, and Neptune"—came straight from the creation science field. The bill, however, did not even make it out of the state house of representatives' education committee. With moderate Republican governor Lamar Alexander touting his education reforms and Tennessee working hard on a technology-friendly "New South" image, few lawmakers wanted another evolution fight.

Things were different eleven years later, however. In the "Republican revolution" of 1994, the governorship of Tennessee, both U.S. Senate seats and control of the state senate passed from Democrats to the GOP. The shift emboldened Christian conservatives in the state and across the country, prompting a variety of religiously inspired legislation. The first sign of this in Tennessee was a proposal to "encourage" the posting of the Ten Commandments in public buildings, including schools. The nonbinding bill passed, despite an opinion from the state attorney general that it would be unconstitutional to carry out its mandate.

Around the same time that bill was under debate, in early 1996, a popular Democratic senator from rural Middle Tennessee took an even bolder step. Tommy Burks, a conservative farmer from Monterey, sponsored Senate

Bill 3229, an act barring the teaching of evolution as "fact" in Tennessee schools. Teachers were instead instructed to discuss the concept only as a "theory." The short piece of legislation offered no definition of either term, one of many issues seized upon by opponents. Burks simply said some constituents had complained to him that their children were being taught evolution against their will.

The reaction in the national media was swift, in part because the so-called religious right, which had been seen as a marginal group in the 1960s and 1970s, had emerged as a national political power. Within weeks, newspapers from California to New York carried stories about the new evolution controversy in Tennessee. None of them failed to mention the Scopes case. A story in the *Chicago Tribune* began, "The state where John Scopes was tried and convicted in 1925 for teaching evolution again wants to restrict what students can be told about the origins of humans."[32] National TV news programs did stories about the bill, drawing in the Ten Commandments legislation as well. Even the British Broadcasting Corporation came to the state to do a report.

In Tennessee itself, public discussion carried strong echoes of the debate that preceded passage of the Butler Act. Most of the state's major newspapers editorialized against the bill (the exception was the *Memphis Commercial-Appeal*, which took no stand; in 1925, the paper had strongly supported the Butler Act).[33] They attacked it for reasons both scientific and economic. The *Nashville Banner*, noting the city's recent recruitment of a professional football team, lamented, "As Tennessee is poised to ride the National Football League to a new level of visibility and prestige, revisiting a 70-year-old melodrama will be counterproductive."[34] The new law was seen by its opponents almost entirely in light of the Scopes case and what they saw as its unfortunate aftermath. An editorial in the *(Nashville) Tennessean* called the bill "crude neanderthal legislation" and continued, "By passing a new Monkey Law and endorsing the Ten Commandments, Tennessee lawmakers are giving the entire state an image of hicks, rubes and yokels."[35]

In contrast, supporters wielded the same God-fearing rhetoric that had helped the Butler Act pass. Rep. Zane Whitson, who sponsored the bill in the house, said those who opposed it "aren't believers like I am. . . . The atheists are opposed to this bill."[36] A few weeks later, during committee debate of the bill, Whitson added, "If people think the state should be embarrassed because of Christians, they should think again."[37]

That stark divide—between "atheists" and "Christians"—typified the way the evolution issue often had been framed in Tennessee politics, and it went a long way toward explaining why it still had so much potency. State Senator Steve Cohen, a Memphis Democrat who was the most outspoken critic of the 1996 bill and also the only Jewish member of the senate at the time, complained, "It's so easy to misrepresent a person's motives in opposing such a bill and make them look as though they're not protecting the Constitution—which you take an oath to do—but like they're against somebody's religion or against God."[38] By positioning themselves as champions of righteousness against the forces of godlessness, anti-evolutionists in Tennessee and elsewhere polarized the issue in a way that caused many legislators to avoid the fight. But those who did oppose it had more allies in 1996 than they had ever had in the state. University faculty from across the state spoke out strongly against it, a marked contrast to the Butler Act. The politically powerful Tennessee Education Association, a teachers' lobbying group that did not exist in 1925 and indeed could not have existed before Peay's education reforms standardized teacher licensing, was also vocal in fighting the proposal. Finally, the state's success in attracting scientists from around the world to facilities at Oak Ridge and elsewhere ensured a large professional base of support for science education.

The Burks bill passed education committee votes in both the house and senate. But by then the tide of negative publicity had started to take a toll. The state attorney general had issued an opinion that the law would be unconstitutional if enforced. And moderate Republican Governor Don Sundquist, who had run on a strong pro-business platform, stayed out of the issue entirely. Cohen told the *Los Angeles Times,* "It makes us look like a backwoods state, a state that discourages educated thinking and science."[39] Even some Christian conservative legislators backed

away, calling the bill's language too vague to be useful. When it finally came to a full senate vote on March 28, it failed by a twenty to thirteen vote. However, like Speaker John Wilder, those who opposed the bill were reluctant to endorse evolution. Sen. Andy Womack, who chaired the senate's education committee and was the sole committee member to vote against the legislation, said, "I tried from the very beginning not to . . . get involved in the issue of evolution itself, but to deal with it as an issue of whether the Legislature should be determining what and how subjects should be taught in school."[40]

Still, the difference in outcome between the passage of the Butler Act and the rejection of the Burks bill can be attributed at least in part to the legacy of the Scopes case. As in 1925, few of the legislators who initially supported the 1996 bill actually felt strongly about the issue; they were, instead, torn between strongly religious constituents and fear of damaging the state's reputation and economic competitiveness. Unlike Austin Peay, however, they had no illusions that the bill would go unchallenged. The Scopes trial had put legislators on notice that even "symbolic" laws could have very real legal consequences, and even more significant cultural ramifications. In 1996, however powerful the religious lobby remained, it was no longer pragmatic politics to vote against evolution.

EDUCATION: AN ONGOING STRUGGLE

Billy Stair has spent more than two decades in and around Tennessee state government, including many years as a key aide and adviser to a popular governor, Ned McWherter. In the 1970s, he left his home state to study at Penn State University. Although that school has much in common with the University of Tennessee—both are large institutions that were established as agricultural land-grant schools—Stair found his Pennsylvania classmates had nothing but scorn for Tennessee. As he later wrote, "I was startled to discover that the general perception of Tennessee education is still, after half a century, a product of the 1925 trial of John Thomas Scopes. . . ."[41]

Stair still thinks the perception is unfair. "Over the last twenty years, there has been far more emotional debate or far more contentious debate of evolution in a number of states, including the North and West, than in Tennessee. And yet if you mention the word evolution, the first association for many people is Tennessee," he said.[42] There is some truth in his assertion. Despite Tennessee's occasional evolution battles, other states have placed more restrictions on their educators. Alabama, for example, requires all textbooks that discuss evolution to carry a disclaimer at the front warning students that evolution is just one of many theories about the origins of man. But there is no way to extricate Tennessee from its place in the Darwin debate, and classroom instruction in the seventy-five years since the Scopes trial reflects that reality.

It is important to understand first of all what kind of "evolution" was being taught in the years before Scopes. The book Scopes—and most Tennessee science teachers—used was George William Hunter's *A Civic Biology*, the leading text in the country. Although evolutionary science itself was still very much evolving in the first decades of the century, some combination of natural selection and genetic variation was understood by most scientists as the basis for diversification of species. Darwin's concepts became especially prominent with the merging of two previous separate fields—botany and zoology—under the umbrella of biology. Texts reflected that prominence; Hunter, a teacher at New York's DeWitt Clinton High School, could hardly have left discussion of evolution out of a modern science book. His textbook called Darwin "the grand old man of biology" and cited his work as the foundation of the modern scientific worldview.[43]

The Scopes case changed that approach, and not just in Tennessee. Scared by the publicity and the possibility of losing sales in states with large fundamentalist populations, textbook publishers started to back away from Darwin. The Hunter book was extensively revised in later editions, dropping the word "evolution" completely and eliminating charts showing the descent of one species from another. General concepts of natural selection remained in most textbooks, but they were left fairly vague. And Hunter's revisions included a sentence affirming that "Man is the only creature that has moral and religious instincts." That did not help it in

Tennessee. In fact, the book was dropped from the state's approved list of texts shortly before the trial.[44] If this led to caution nationwide in the teaching of evolution, that caution was most pronounced in areas where teachers were most worried about offending parents and school board members, which included most of the South and, inevitably, Tennessee. Within a few decades of the Scopes trial, said Ronald Numbers, "The teaching of evolution had withered."[45]

If any science teachers in Tennessee were looking to the state's largest educational institution for help during this period, they were surely disappointed. The University of Tennessee, dependent on funding from the state legislature, assiduously avoided the controversy. During debate over the Butler Act, university president Harcourt A. Morgan—himself a botanist and former dean of the university's agriculture school—privately urged Governor Peay to veto it but took no public stand. Like Peay, he was more concerned about improvements to the overall education system than one contentious law. His prudence arguably paid off; the same legislature that passed the Butler Act appropriated more than a million dollars in capital funding for the university.[46] Only one faculty member, Nathan Dougherty of the College of Engineering, actively opposed the law.

In 1951, Tennessee created a State Textbook Commission to "prepare a list of approved standard editions of textbooks for use in the public schools."[47] The seven-member board, made up of teachers and school administrators from across the state, was given the job of certifying texts in all subjects, with each major academic area—science, history, literature, etc.—coming up for review every four years. All proposed texts were presented for public review and comment. Although the commission's records are extremely sketchy, it appears that evolution was not a topic of controversy in the board's early years—a phenomenon possibly attributable to the lack of emphasis many texts placed on it.

As with so much else in American schools, however, the treatment of Darwin began to change in 1957, after the launch of the Russian Sputnik satellite. Suddenly nuts-and-bolts science education was a top national priority. A government-sponsored group of scientists and teachers organized the Biological Sciences Curriculum Study, which called for—among other things—a much greater and more detailed emphasis on evolutionary concepts. The group's slogan, adopted to recognize the 1959 centenary of the publication of Darwin's *Origin of Species,* was "100 years without evolution is enough."[48] When new textbooks came out that reflected the BSCS recommendations, they were adopted by schools across the country—even in Tennessee, where they were still technically illegal under the Butler Act.[49]

In fact, some of the state's science educators were increasingly uneasy about the persistence of the 1925 law on the books. Although there had been no further prosecutions, the mere possibility of a teacher or professor being censured for dutifully teaching their subject area both worried and angered them. Faculty members at the University of Tennessee, in decided contrast to their reticence forty years earlier, were in the vanguard of the effort to repeal the old "monkey law." Academic Vice-President Herman Spivey, who helped build the university's relationship with Oak Ridge National Laboratory, lent his support, as did Arthur W. Jones of the department of zoology. University of Tennessee Vice President Edward J. Boling, who later became the university's president, lobbied the legislature in Nashville for the law's repeal.[50]

Shortly after that successful effort , however, anti-evolution groups began seeking redress in the state's classrooms. Russell Artist, the creation scientist who would ultimately prompt the 1973 "equal time" bill, first made his appeal to the State Textbook Commission. On July 13, 1970, Artist led a delegation to the commission's summer meeting to protest science books proposed for adoption, on the grounds that they ignored alternatives to Darwinian evolution. He also "requested that the commission examine a forthcoming textbook in biology written with a more conservative or Christian concept of creation"[51] But because the creationist book Artist referred to (and co-wrote) had not actually been published yet, the commission rejected it. Later, after the 1973 law had passed, the commission did add the book to its approved list, as a "supplementary text" available to interested teachers.[52]

Since then, evolution has been taught to one degree or another in Tennessee schools.

Books currently used in Tennessee—all of them published nationally—include long and detailed sections on Darwin, natural selection, and different models of evolution. For example, a text called *Biology: The Dynamics of Life*, published by McGraw-Hill in 1998, tells students, "all of the structures, behaviors, interactions, and internal processes observed in the millions of species of organisms on Earth are the result of the process of evolution."[53] The same book has an entire chapter on "Primate Evolution," which concludes: "Most anthropologists now agree that modern *Homo sapiens* evolved in Africa and spread from Africa throughout the rest of the world."[54] There is no mention of controversy over the concept of evolution or of creation science. But even if defenders of Tennessee's schools say evolution is taught here as it is anywhere, there are signs of lingering discomfort.

In March 1998, the Thomas B. Fordham Foundation in Washington, D.C., issued a report on science education standards across the country. Dr. Lawrence S. Lerner, a professor of physics at California State University—Long Beach, reviewed science requirements in thirty-six states and issued each a grade based on their rigor, clarity, and specificity. One key criterion for Lerner was whether the "basic underlying principles of all the sciences are stressed," including "evolution and the molecular basis of life in biology."[55] To his dismay, Lerner found that the latter subject in particular was lacking in several states—mostly in the South. He noted that Arizona, Florida, Georgia, Kentucky, and South Carolina all danced around the issue of human evolution in their curricula. He also noted Alabama's textbook disclaimer law. But he found two states where evolution simply did not appear in state guidelines at all— Mississippi and Tennessee. In his report card for Tennessee, Lerner lamented general vagueness in the curriculum and then concluded with a very specific complaint: "Most embarrassing of all, however, is the fact that the treatment of biology in Tennessee seems not to have changed since the notorious 'Monkey Trial' of 1925. Biological evolution is not merely euphemized, as is a widespread practice in Southern states, but it is entirely absent. Moreover, geological evolution is slighted and cosmological evolution completely ignored."[56] His overall grade for the state's standards: F.

Linda Jordan, for many years Tennessee's secondary science curriculum director, said Lerner's critique was at least partly right. Although she said the basic concepts of evolution are part of the state's guidelines, she acknowledges the word "evolution" was left out for primarily political reasons in order to get the curriculum approved by the legislature: "They were afraid that the whole [document] would be blown out of the water." As of this writing, the state is developing an end-of-course test for all high school biology students, and Jordan said evolutionary concepts will figure heavily in it. A former classroom teacher herself, she said, "Any good biology teacher that I know includes [evolution]. Whether it's against their fundamental beliefs or not, they'll teach that to some degree." On the other hand, she admits that political pressures, especially in more rural, religiously homogeneous school districts, do discourage some teachers from going into much detail about Darwinian concepts: "If a few members of the school board in a small rural area don't want you to do that, then I'm sure you don't do that if you want to keep your job. We just don't know how widespread that is."[57]

Dr. Claudia Melear, an associate professor of education at the University of Tennessee in Knoxville, is familiar with the problem. A teacher of students who want to be science teachers, she said about half of them expressed some concern about how to approach evolution because of their own religious convictions. Moreover, she said, they often come to her graduate-level classes without a good background in the subject. "I would say 75 percent of them say they were not taught evolution," Melear said. But she noted the same is true in many states, not just in Tennessee. When she was starting out as a biology teacher in Georgia, she was often alone among her colleagues in being willing to teach the topic. And when she sends her students out on teaching internships, she said, "My interns have told me over the years what their teachers say to them; they say, 'It's too controversial. I can't deal with the parents. I just leave it out.'"[58]

As in the political realm, though, the balance in Tennessee education may be tilting away from the anti-evolution forces. Linda Jordan, for one, promises the state's department of education will address it head-on the next time it revisits its science standards. "When that comes up for revision in 2003, I assure you we won't duck the issue again," she says, "not after the criticism we got from Fordham." And Melear thinks rising activism from the higher-education ranks bodes well. That activism seems to be reflected at the University of Tennessee. During debate of the 1996 anti-evolution bill, university professors spoke out to legislators and in the media not only opposing the proposed law but strongly supporting the teaching of evolution (a step many legislators were unwilling to take). The year after the Burks bill failed, a group of scientists and educators began organizing annual events on Darwin's birthday each February to promote the teaching of evolution. The events, dubbed "Darwin Day," usually include workshops for schoolteachers with educational and legal resources. "The increase in knowledge and interest in teaching evolution is directly related to scientists' involvement," Melear says. "That's the key."

Every summer, the town of Dayton hosts reenactments of the Scopes trial. The Rhea

County Courthouse has changed very little since 1925, and spectators can sit in the same chairs the original crowds did and watch the drama unfold before the same judicial bench. It's a tourist attraction and awakens a bit of nostalgia as well—a chance for the still small town to remember the summer when it played host to the world. A modest museum in the basement of the courthouse gathers photographs and memorabilia from the trial, along with newspaper clippings from around the country.

But if Dayton enjoys its odd place in history, it's also clear the town is not exactly anxious for that kind of attention again. It may be representative of Tennessee as a whole, in that sense. As the state has struggled to grasp the long-term consequences of the summer of 1925, it seems to have reached a conclusion that the less said about it, the better. In 1996, during the debate of the most recent anti-evolution bill, the principal of Dayton's Rhea County High School told his biology teachers not to make any public comments about the legislation. "We have nothing to gain by what we might say," Principal Patrick Conner said. "We don't want to start another Scopes trial."[59]

Notes

Introduction

1. This theme is fully developed in Edward J. Larson, *Summer for the Gods: The Scopes Trial and America's Continuing Debate over Science and Religion* (New York: Basic Books, 1997).

2. William Jennings Bryan to Florida State Senator W. J. Singleton, 11 Apr. 1922; W. J. Bryan Papers, Library of Congress, Washington, D.C.

3. Ray Ginger, *Six Days or Forever? Tennessee v. John Thomas Scopes* (New York: Oxford University Press, 1958), 5–6.

4. Robert E. Corlew, *Tennessee: A Short History,* 2d ed. (Knoxville: The University of Tennessee Press, 1981).

5. Ginger, *Six Days,* 2–3.

6. Ibid., 3–4.

7. Butler explained his rationale in "Dayton's 'Amazing' Trial," *Literary Digest* 86, 25 July 1925, 7.

8. Thomas Page Gore to editor, *(Nashville) Tennessean,* 1 Feb. 1925, 4.

9. "Proceedings in Legislature," *(Nashville) Tennessean,* 11 Mar. 1925, 8.

10. For details on passage of the bill, see Kenneth K. Bailey, "The Enactment of Tennessee's Anti-evolution Law," *Journal of Southern History* 16 (1) (1950): 472–90.

11. Austin Peay, "Messages from the Governor," 23 Mar. 1925, *Journal of the House of Representatives of Tennessee* (1925 Reg. Sess.), 741–45.

12. "Cries at Restrictive Law," *New York Times,* 26 Apr. 1925; ACLU Archives, Princeton Univ. Libraries, Princeton, N.J., vol. 273.

13. Ginger, *Six Days,* 70–71.

14. "Doubts Legality of Special Term," *Chattanooga Times,* 24 May 1925, 9.

15. Ginger, *Six Days,* 19–20, 69.

16. "Evolution Taught at Central High," *Chattanooga Times,* 19 May 1925, 5.

17. "Dayton Jolly as Evolution Trial Looms," *Chattanooga Times*, 21 May 1925, 1; "Dayton to Raise Advertising Fund," *Chattanooga Times*, 23 May 1925, 15.

18. "Darrow Likens Bryan to Nero," *Nashville Banner*, 18 May 1925, 1.

19. W. H. Pitkin to Felix Frankfurter, 10 Nov. 1926, ACLU Archives, vol. 299.

20. Ginger, *Six Days*, 216.

21. In *Clarence Darrow: The Story of My Life* (New York: Gosset, 1932), Darrow states, "My object was to focus the attention of the country on the programme of Mr. Bryan and the other fundamentalists in America" (249).

22. Will Herberg, *Protestant, Catholic, Jew* (Garden City, N.J.: Doubleday, 1960), 259–60.

23. Darrow, *The Story of My Life*, p. 409. Clarence Darrow, "Why I am an Agnostic," in Clarence Darrow, *Verdicts Out of Court*, Arthur Weinburg and Lil Weinberg, eds. (Chicago: Quadrangle, 1963), p.434.

24. George E. Webb, *The Evolution Controversy in America* (Lexington: Univ. Press of Kentucky, 1994), 62–67.

25. William Jennings Bryan, "The Prince of Peace," in *Speeches of William Jennings Bryan*, ed. Bryan (New York: Funk & Wagnalls, 1909), 266–68.

26. Lawrence W. Levine, *Defender of the Faith: William Jennings Bryan: The Last Decade, 1915–1925* (New York: Oxford Univ. Press, 1965), 261–62.

27. Ibid., 261–70.

28. Webb, *The Evolution Controversy*, 68–69.

29. Quoted in Ginger, *Six Days*, 35.

30. Bryan, "Prince of Peace," 268–69.

31. William Jennings Bryan, "W.G.N. Put 'on Carpet,' Gets Bryan Lashing," *Chicago Tribune*, 20 June 1923, 14.

32. William Jennings Bryan, *In His Image* (New York: Revell, 1922), 103–4.

33. Ibid., 94.

34. Leslie H. Allen, ed., *Bryan and Darrow at Dayton: The Record and Documents of the "Bible-Evolution Trial"* (New York: Russell & Russell, 1925, 1967), 173.

35. Ibid., 177.

36. Ginger, *Six Days*, 21.

37. Ference Morton Szasz, *The Divided Mind of Protestant America, 1880–1930* (University: Univ. of Alabama Press, 1982), 92.

38. Ibid., 131–32.

39. William Jennings Bryan, "Speech to Legislature," in Bryan, *Orthodox Christianity Versus Modernism* (New York: Revell, 1923), 46.

40. William Jennings Bryan, *Is the Bible True?* (Nashville: Private printing, 1923), 15.

41. On the ACLU history and civil liberties, see James Harvey Robinson, *The Mind in the Making: The Relation of Intellect to Social Reform* (New York: Harper, 1921); Samuel Walker, *In Defense of American Liberties: A History of the ACLU* (New York: Oxford Univ. Press, 1990).

42. Roger N. Baldwin, "Dayton's first Issue," in Jerry R. Tompkins, ed., *D-Days at Dayton: Reflections of the Scopes Trial* (Baton Rouge: Louisiana State Univ. Press, 1965), 56.

43. Ginger, *Six Days*, 106.

44. Ibid., 120–21.

45. Ibid., 124–25.

46. Quoted in Larson, *Summer for the Gods,* 177–80.

47. Allen, *Bryan and Darrow,* 138–39, 145–46, 153–54.

48. Ginger, *Six Days,* 192–93.

49. Quoted in Larson, *Summer for the Gods,* 200.

50. Stanley J. Folmsbee, Robert E. Corlew, Enoch L. Mitchell, *History of Tennessee* (New York: Lewis Historical Publishing Co., Inc., 1960), 280.

51. Ginger, *Six Days,* 212–13.

52. Larson, *Summer for the Gods,* 237–38.

53. Corlew, *Tennessee,* 544.

54. Tenn. Code Ann. sec. 49-2008; Ark. Stat. Ann. sec. 80-1663, et. sec. (1981 Supp.); La. Rev. Stat. Ann. sec. 17: 286.3 (1981); For a complete discussion of these statutes and the litigation they spawned, see Edward J. Larson, *Trial and Error: The American Controversy Over Creation and Evolution* (New York: Oxford Univ. Press, 1989), 125–88.

55. *(Nashville) Tennessean,* Mar. 21, 1996, A1.

56. *Nashville Banner,* Mar. 28, 1996, A1.

57. Folmsbee, Corlew, and Mitchell, *History of Tennessee,* 280.

Afterword

1. Larry Daughtrey, *(Nashville) Tennessean,* 29 Mar. 1996, A1.

2. Herman A. Norton, *Religion in Tennessee 1777–1945* (Knoxville: Univ. of Tennessee Press, 1981), 4–8.

3. Ibid., 8–10.

4. Ibid., 28.

5. Ibid., 53.

6. Ibid., 81.

7. Ibid., 80.

8. Edward J. Larson, *Summer for the Gods: The Scopes Trial and America's Continuing Debate over Science and Religion* (New York: Basic Books, 1997), 20.

9. Ibid., 23.

10. Ibid., 43.

11. Joel A. Carpenter, *Revive Us Again: The Reawakening of American Fundamentalism* (New York: Oxford Univ. Press, 1997), 33.

12. Larson, *Summer for the Gods,* 183.

13. Ibid., 233.

14. Ibid., 237.

15. Orland Kay Armstrong, "Bootleg Science in Tennessee," *North American Review* 227 (Feb. 1929): 140.

16. Ronald Numbers, *The Creationists: The Evolution of Scientific Creationism* (New York: Knopf, 1992), 81.

17. Ronald Numbers, interview with Jesse Fox Mayshark, May 1998.

18. Numbers, The Creationists, 233.

19. Kurt Wise, interview with Jesse Fox Mayshark, Apr. 1998.

20. Billy Stair, "Religion, Politics, and the Myth of Tennessee Education," *Tennessee Teacher* 95 (Apr. 1978): 20.

21. Stanley J. Folmsbee, et al. *Tennessee: A Short History* (Knoxville: Univ. of Tennessee Press, 1969), 456.

22. Paul H. Bergeron, *Paths of the Past: Tennessee, 1770–1970* (Knoxville: Univ. of Tennessee Press, 1979), 92.

23. Larson, *Summer for the Gods*, 52.

24. Ibid., 48.

25. Ibid., 59.

26. Ibid., 250.

27. Ibid., 253.

28. Edward J. Larson, *Trial and Error: The American Controversy Over Creation and Evolution* (Oxford Univ. Press, 1989), 134.

29. Record of the Tennessee House of Representatives, 26 Apr. 1973, 1156–57.

30. Ibid.

31. "Fundamental Setback for Fundamentalists," *Science* 188 (2 May 1975), 428.

32. *Chicago Tribune*, 5 Mar. 1996, A10.

33. Larson, *Summer for the Gods*, 48.

34. *Nashville Banner*, 4 Mar. 1996, A10.

35. *(Nashville) Tennessean*, 26 Feb. 1996, A10.

36. *Nashville Banner*, 22 Feb. 1996, A1.

37. *Memphis Commercial Appeal*, 6 Mar. 1996, A1.

38. Steve Cohen, interview with Jesse Fox Mayshark, Nov. 1998.

39. *Los Angeles Times*, 31 Mar. 1996, A6.

40. Cynthia A. McCune, "Framing Reality: Shaping News Coverage of the 1996 Tennessee Debate on Evolution," (Master's thesis, San Jose State Univ., 1998), 77.

41. Stair, "Religion, Politics," 17–18.

42. Billy Stair, interview with Jesse Fox Mayshark, Dec. 1998.

43. Larson, *Summer for the Gods*, 23–24.

44. Ibid., 231.

45. Numbers, interview.

46. James Riley Montgomery, et al. *To Foster Knowledge: A History of the University of Tennessee, 1794–1970* (Knoxville: Univ. of Tennessee Press, 1984), 189.

47. Tennessee Code Annotated, Sec. 49-2008 (1956).

48. Numbers, interview.

49. Larson, *Summer for the Gods*, 249.

50. Montgomery, *To Foster Knowledge*, 278.

51. Minutes of the Meeting of the Tennessee State Textbook Commission, July 13, 1970, p. 3.

52. Dorothy Thompson Weathersby, "Censorship of Literature Textbooks in Tennessee: A Study of the Commission, Publishers, Teachers, and Textbooks," (Ph.D. diss., Univ. of Tennessee, 1975), 86.

53. Alton Biggs, et al. *Biology: The Dynamics of Life* (New York: McGraw-Hill, 1998), 20.

54. Ibid., 474.

55. Lawrence Lerner, "State Science Standards: An Appraisal of Science Standards in 36 States," Thomas B. Fordham Foundation, March 1998, 4.

56. Ibid., 28.

57. Linda Jordan, interview with Jesse Fox Mayshark, Jan. 1999.

58. Claudia Melear, interview with Jesse Fox Mayshark, Feb. 1999.

59. *Seattle Times*, 13 Mar. 1996, A3.